The Book
of Balloons

ERIK NØRGAARD

The Book of
Balloons

Translated and revised by Erik Hildesheim

Crown Publishers, Inc.   New York

FRONT ENDPAPER: *Section of a print showing the first balloon ascension undertaken in Strasbourg on May 15, 1784. The pilot is the Frenchman Adorne. The name of the passenger is unknown.*

REAR ENDPAPER: *Part of a print showing the English balloon pilot James Sadler during an ascension from Oxford on July 7, 1810. Sadler made his first flight in 1784. He made numerous other ascensions before he died in 1828.*

JACKET (FRONT): *Participants in an Alpine balloon rally in Mürren, Switzerland, in 1964, are shown crossing the mountains.* (BACK): *An imaginary balloon project from the beginning of the nineteenth century.*

OPPOSITE: *Three Englishmen—Alan Root, Douglas Botting, and Anthony Smith, the last being the organizer and pilot of the expedition—in 1962 made a balloon trip from Zanzibar across the African continent to the Serengeti Reservation. One of their aims was taking moving pictures of the wildlife from their silent aircraft. The balloon, named "Jambo," was photographed in the air over Africa. Anthony Smith's book* Jambo *tells of their trip.*

Originally published in Danish in 1970 as DEN GIK ALLIGEVEL, GRANBERG

© 1970 by Erik Nøgraard and Lademann Publishing House, Inc.
English translation © 1971 by Crown Publishers, Inc.

Library of Congress Catalog Card Number: 73–147322
Printed in Czechoslovakia by Svoboda, Prague

This book is dedicated to the memory of the sailor prince who, during the siege of Paris in 1870, climbed aboard the balloon "Jacquard" and remarked: "Now I begin the greatest trip of my life. This air voyage will be talked about everywhere!" The balloon ascended, soared away above the heads of the Prussian soldiers, continued across France—and out to sea over the Atlantic.

The prince was never seen again.

Foreword

This book deals with one of the most significant milestones in history—man's first successful device for leaving the ground and traveling in the air, many centuries after he had mastered traveling on the oceans. It is also a tale of failures and unfulfilled expectations.

For a full century after balloons first rose in the air—in due course, after they had assumed an elongated and reinforced shape, they would be called airships—it was hoped they would be vehicles that could cover the greatest distances in the world by air, rapidly and safely. This was not to be the case. In time, we succeeded in making the airship rigid and independent of the direction of the wind, but in the long run it was unable to compete successfully with the speedier and more reliable airplane.

The balloon, however, has never relinquished its hold on our imagination. Though it is thrilling to view jet aircraft and moon rockets in their skybound leaps, it remains as fascinating as ever to watch the balloon, man's oldest aircraft, rise silently and soar away.

Many countries played a part in the history of the balloon. It was in France that animals and human beings first took off and broke their bondage to earth. England soon afterward founded a proud balloon tradition of her own. Elsewhere, too, balloon pilots and airship crews set out on dangerous and bold—some said foolhardy—adventures. Even small countries like Denmark and Holland have similar heroes of their own. Germany took the lead with Zeppelins, which for a while were believed to be the air vehicle of the future for both war and peace.

This volume is not a technical report. First and foremost, it treats the subject pictorially and is a tale of true adventures. It also deals with the romance and beauty of the balloon and relates stories of daring aeronauts, their triumphs and tragedies.

Erik Nørgaard

The Dream of Flying Like the Birds

Man mastered the wheel and thereby could travel on land at speeds previously unheard of. He built ships and could navigate the waters safely. Then he looked skyward and watched the birds. Why should he not be able to learn to fly too?

The dream of flying like the birds has always been with us. The earliest civilizations left evidence of dreaming about leaving the ground and soaring away in the air. But the dream remained only a dream. In spite of numerous attempts, no one succeeded in duplicating the performance of the birds. Only in mythology was the impossible possible. The gods of old possessed superhuman powers, one of which was their ability to fly. And in the Christian faith both God's selected children (the angels) and the evil spirit (the devil himself) were equipped with wings.

One of the oldest legends about an ordinary man being able to fly concerns the Greek artisan Daedalus and his son Icarus. Daedalus worked in Athens, but he became involved in a manslaughter suit and had to escape to Crete. There, King Minos entrusted him with the erection of a giant labyrinth, and Daedalus completed that job to the king's satisfaction. But then he gave the king's daughter Ariadne the secret of the labyrinth so that she could help Theseus, whom she loved, to escape from it. Enraged at Daedalus, the king had him imprisoned in the very labyrinth he himself had constructed. Daedalus's knowledge of the pathways to freedom did him no good—all exits were guarded by sentinels. He must find another way to escape.

A drawing of the legendary flight of Daedalus and Icarus.

In 1680, the Italian professor Giovanni Borelli rendered a scientifically correct description of the basic physical laws governing the flight of birds and explained the conditions man must fulfill to fly like them. These prerequisites are incapable of being met.

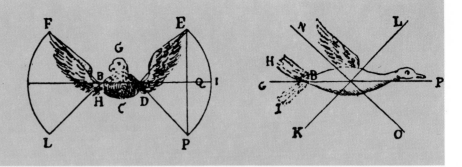

Right: *The devil himself wears wings in this etching by Eugène Delacroix.*

Cupid's costume, in a Paris opera from 1710—another expression of man's dream of flying.

At length, Daedalus had a brilliant idea. Perhaps he could escape by air—it might be possible to fly away like a bird. He managed to procure some feathers and proceeded to make pairs of wings for himself and his son Icarus, fastening them to their bodies with wax.

The idea worked. Father and son found they could indeed fly. The puzzled sentinels guarding them watched in astonishment, unable to prevent their escape.

At first, it looked as if the two would reach the mainland safely. Young Icarus, however, became too daring. In spite of his father's warnings, he flew too close to the sun and the wax on his wings began to melt. Then his wings dropped off completely and he plunged to his death in the ocean, which later—and until recent years—was called the Icarian Sea. Daedalus himself maintained an ample distance from the sun and was able to land on the mainland.

A number of optimistic inventors truly believed that the solution to flight would be found in imitating the birds, but all of them were to be disappointed.

How to Create the Flying Man

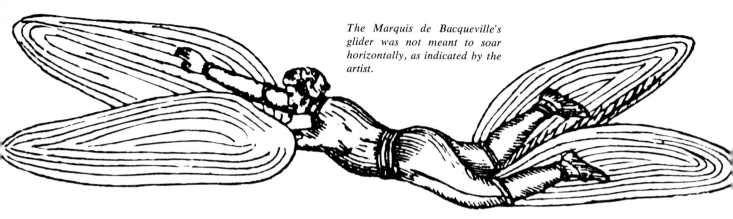

The Marquis de Bacqueville's glider was not meant to soar horizontally, as indicated by the artist.

Gradually it became an accepted fact that human beings cannot fly simply by copying the wings of birds and using them to rise. Many who pondered the tantalizing problem felt inclined to agree with the words of an Indian sage: "If God had meant us to fly, he would have provided us with wings."

But man is indomitable. The idea of flying haunted him, and keen and inspired minds kept searching for an answer. Those who attacked the problem in a practical manner realized that there must be a different approach—some mechanical device was required.

The universally brilliant Leonardo da Vinci (1452–1519) had already conceived several ideas for "flying machines" incorporating mechanical means. For example, he sketched a framework to hold the human body and fitted it with an elevator control, which he foresaw would be necessary for climbing and descending. The "machine" was to be propelled by foot power—Leonardo knew the leg muscles are the strongest ones in man's body (see sketch on page 14). Another of his aircraft was, in principle, a precursor of today's helicopter. Da Vinci noted: "If a screw [propeller] is turned at sufficient speed it will provide the lift required for the craft to take off." His observations were correct. The only drawback was the lack of a power source to drive the screw,

Flying apparatus of the Vienna tailor, Degen. Unable to produce enough leg power to rise, he later used the lift power of a balloon.

Locksmith Besnier with his idea for flying. Once more, the aritst depicts greater success than was actually achieved.

2

An illustration from a novel by Rétif de la Bretonne (1734–1806). An industrious author, he could turn out a novel in one week Most of his stories gave evidence of his vivid imagination. The picture below, from his tale about Victorin, shows the hero as he carries the belle Christine away across the roofs of the city. Victorin's winged dress serves as a parachute.

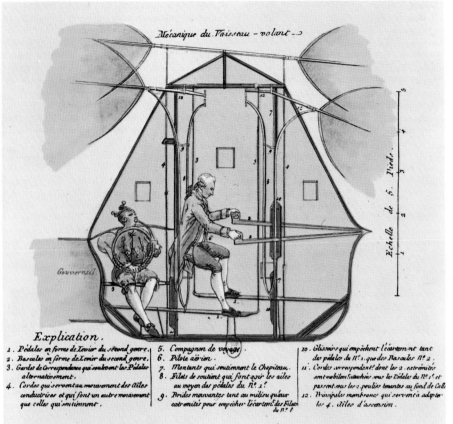

one that would not be too heavy.

Others studying the problem of flight stuck mainly to the glider idea.

In 1659 the Marquis of Worcester took out a patent about which he wrote:

"How to produce a flying man. I have experimented with a ten-year-old boy in a barn, after first padding the floor with hay." Nothing has been learned about a practical exploitation of this patent, but it is a safe bet that the youngster survived because of the precaution of spreading hay on the floor.

The Belgian locksmith Besnier was another air pioneer. He constructed an apparatus with four wings that spread out on the downstroke and folded when raised. Besnier is reported to have suc-ceeded in some kind of soaring with his glider.

In 1742, work on the aircraft conceived and built by the Marquis de Bacqueville had advanced to the stage where he could invite the public to attend an aerial crossing of the Seine. Evidently he lacked the courage of his convictions and doubted that his invention was perfect, for he told his butler to man the aircraft. This butler not only was cautious, but a born diplomat as well. He expressed implicit faith in the excellence of the aircraft, but added that it would be wrong of him to deprive his master of the honor of being the first to rise in it. The marquis, susceptible to flattery, realized that his servant had spoken words of wisdom, so he went ahead himself.

But his aircraft was far from perfect. He plunged into the river and broke both his legs.

By now it seemed to be conclusively proved that man was incapable of rising from the ground, so the astronomer Joseph de Lalande, a member of the French Academy of Sciences, passed this verdict on the dream of flying: "Now it has been proved beyond the shadow of a doubt that not only is it impossible for us to fly by means of artificial wings, but also—once in the air—to stay there. Man has been created to remain on the ground, the winged creatures to gambol above us. Do not let us waste our time by trying to alter the basic laws of nature." However, Lalande was not to have the final word!

1

On the Track of a Solution

Cyrano de Bergerac suggested several means of air travel and of reaching distant planets. One was by outfitting each person with small balls from which the air had been removed and replaced with dew, which could be heated by the sun. Another placed passengers in an airship shaped like a wardrobe and fitted with a large ball and sail. The wind would blow against the sail, thereby driving the craft forward. In this case also the ball would be filled with dew to be heated by the sun.

Among the many who endeavored to master the element of the birds was the previously mentioned Italian scientist Giovanni Alfonso Borelli. His was the nearest approach to a temporary solution. In 1680 he quoted Archimedes' principle: "A body submerged in water is supported by a force equal to the weight of the water it displaces." Borelli went on, "In order to permit a small piece of lead to float, I attach it to a large piece of cork. . . . Fish can remain in equilibrium in water because nature has outfitted them with a large bladder containing air. How is it, then, that nobody ever thought of attaching a practically empty vacuum tank to the human body in order to permit man to float in space in this manner?"

There were, indeed, a few who had thought of this scheme, although they had not expressed their thoughts quite as clearly as Borelli. One was Cyrano de Bergerac, who in two of his books—*The Amusing History of the Lands and Empires on the Moon* and an unfinished one entitled *The Lands and Empires on the Sun*—described travels to other planets by means of, among other things, vacuum balls containing dew only, which was heated by the sun and thereby became lighter than the surrounding air.

Another inventor on the same track—to a still higher degree he anticipated the basic idea of the balloon—was the Jesuit father Francesco de Lana (1631–1687), who outlined several "airships" to be launched by means of vacuum balls. None was actually built, however, and the inventive Father perhaps made a virtue of necessity when he exclaimed, "God would never forgive mankind that such a machine was invented and could be used in times of war to cause untold destruction and misery!"

The name of the Brazilian Bartholemeu de Gusmão should also be mentioned because he lays claim to being the first aeronaut on record. This seems more than doubtful when one studies the drawings of the aircraft he is reported to have operated. Some people maintain that John V of Portugal granted Gusmão an exclusive franchise for the building of aircraft to be used in carrying passengers and merchandise to the Portuguese colonies. His first successful ascension is reported to have occurred on August 8, 1709, in the presence of the royal court.

Whether this be true or not, in the eighteenth century several people had the right idea about one way of solving the problem of travel in the air—by means of the lighter-than-air principle.

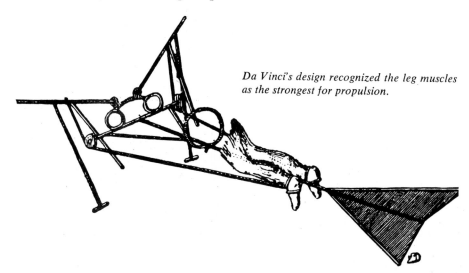

Da Vinci's design recognized the leg muscles as the strongest for propulsion.

Here are two versions of the airship of the Jesuit Father de Lana. The craft above is borne by four vacuum balls. The good Father serenely enjoys his pipe while being paddled through the air. The German illustration at right pictures another version with six vacuum balls, and also depicts space travel as it was envisioned then. The observers on the earth have a difficult time figuring out what they are viewing. Having left the moon behind him, de Lana has climbed above the clouds, and is seen encountering an ambassador from the outer world.

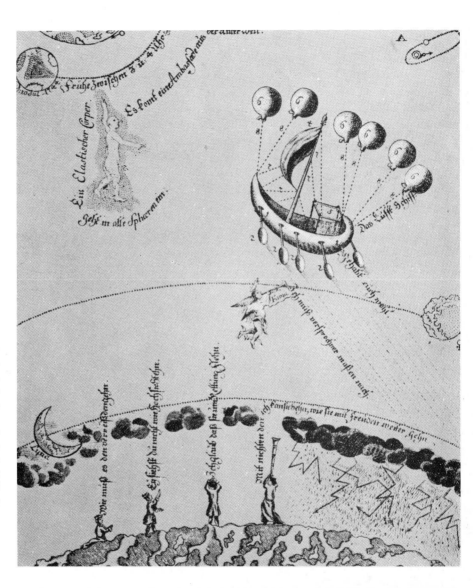

This is what Gusmão's airship looked like, according to a handbill distributed in Vienna in 1709. Gusmão conceived of employing a system of pipes, and also balls of amber, which he claimed had a lift effect, as well as sail power for propulsion. To ensure success, he planned to provide his craft with additional "electrical and magnetic power."

The First Balloon Is Launched

The honor of building the first balloon belongs to two brothers, Joseph and Étienne Montgolfier, of Annonay, a town in southern France. They were the sons of a wealthy paper manufacturer, and even at an early age they were interested in scientific problems.

Joseph especially pondered the puzzling problem of air travel, and experimented with parachutes and mechanical flying devices. Gradually it dawned on him that the solution lay in the lighter-than-air principle. All along, it had been almost self-evident that if one could produce a sufficiently light container and fill it with a gas lighter than the surrounding air, the outcome would be that the container must rise from the ground.

Étienne had been pursuing a promising career as an architect in Paris, but he gave it up and returned to join his brother, so that they could concentrate on the problem and see it through to success.

It appears that the most decisive experiments took place while Joseph Montgolfier stayed alone in Avignon, for it was from that city in 1782 that Joseph, then forty-two, wrote to the younger Étienne, thirty-seven: "Procure me immediately some taffeta and rope, and I will show you something that will astonish the world!" Thus, Joseph must by then have discovered what had challenged many minds for a great many years: the basic principle of the hot-air balloon.

Like many other inventions, this one was really very simple. Joseph Montgolfier merely built small, internally heated, paper balloons to prove that they would rise.

The balloon ascension at Annonay caused great excitement. For the first time man had succeeded in launching a vehicle into the air and keeping it there —at least for ten minutes.

The Montgolfier brothers, Étienne and Joseph.

Opposite: *The first balloon is sent up at Annonay.*

It has been widely theorized that Joseph was guided onto the right track by observing how the smoke rose from the chimneys in Avignon and whirled small particles of ashes skyward. Most historians of aeronautics surmise that both Étienne and Joseph believed smoke to contain a special "electrical quality gas." This is unlikely. No doubt the two brothers realized that it was only the heated air, made lighter, that made the balloon rise.

Scientifically bent as their minds were, the Montgolfier brothers must be supposed to have heard of Cavendish's discovery of the new "water-gas" (hydrogen), which was one-fourteenth the weight of atmospheric air. It would seem more natural for them to have filled their balloons with "water-gas" than by heating them over an open fire. However, it was complicated and costly to produce hydrogen; it also proved difficult to achieve a light and gas-tight balloon cover.

In any event, the brothers continued their experiments, heating paper balloons up to 700 cubic feet in size. Not until the following year did they use the cordage and taffeta Joseph had asked for in 1782. In the spring of 1783 they produced their largest balloon to date, made of so-called wrapping canvas. On Monday, June 5, of that year, the day arrived when they were able to launch a balloon in public from the square in Annonay. This balloon was probably tied to hold it over an open fire. When the air inside the balloon had been heated, the ties were cut—and the balloon rose in the summer sky, where it continued to float for ten minutes, until the hot air cooled. Then it descended.

17

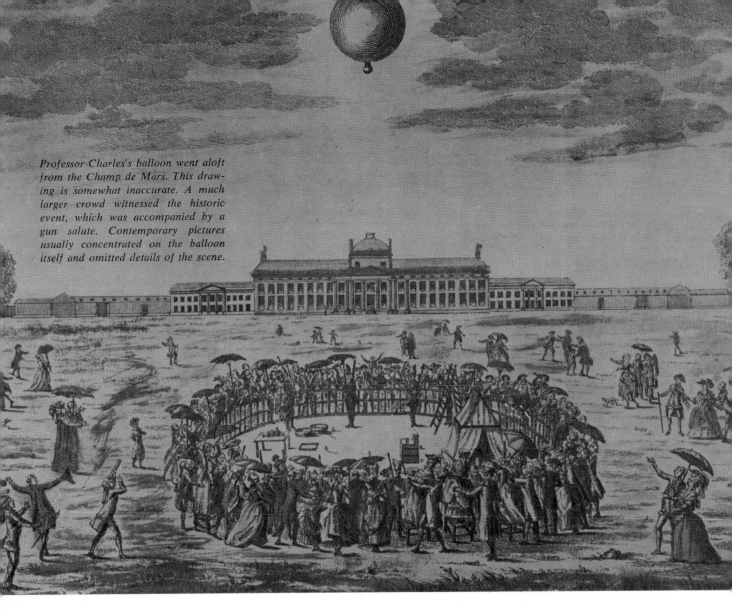

Professor Charles's balloon went aloft from the Champ de Mars. This drawing is somewhat inaccurate. A much larger crowd witnessed the historic event, which was accompanied by a gun salute. Contemporary pictures usually concentrated on the balloon itself and omitted details of the scene.

Professor Charles.

The Cat Is Let Out of the Bag

Rumors about what was going on in Annonay spread rapidly across France, and the Academy of Sciences in Paris decided to look into this invention. Professor Jacques Charles, one of the best-known physicists of the day, and two clever mechanics, the brothers Charles and M. N. Robert, were entrusted with the task. Their model of a balloon was a remarkable accomplishment. (The type became known as a Charlière.) It was practically perfect right from the first, and the type remains in use today in almost its original form. Only in minor details have improvements been added.

It is said that the Montgolfier brothers furnished the Academy a detailed report about their balloon but kept silent about the most important detail—their secret "lift" source, heated air, which made the balloon rise. This undoubtedly is just a story, for the Montgolfiers could scarcely hide the fact that they had started an open fire under their balloon, and Professor Charles would certainly have been able to deduct what actually took place. However, he decided not to proceed along the same lines. He too must have read about the "water-gas" that was fourteen times lighter than atmospheric air, and so with the facilities available to him, it was only natural that he decided to take

The first gas-filled balloon landed in Gonesse and was promptly attacked by the villagers as some sort of monster out of the skies.

Filling the first balloon of Professor Charles with hydrogen in the workshop of the Robert brothers in Paris. It was not only a slow and expensive process, but also a difficult one. The air was saturated with sulfuric fumes, which kept escaping from the barrel, and the heat developed was greater than expected.

advantage of this important quality of the recently discovered gas.

When the balloon was completed, they proceeded with the production of hydrogen by placing a barrel below the balloon and partly filling it with iron shavings and water. Then sulfuric acid was added. The hydrogen that was produced was guided through a heavy leather hose into the balloon. The whole operation proved to be no easy procedure.

They did not dare launch any human beings into the air at first—this balloon was to carry only its own weight. Yet one ton of iron shavings and a half-ton of diluted sulfuric acid were consumed before sufficient hydrogen was produced.

Finally, on August 27, 1783—less than two months after the balloon went aloft in Annonay—Professor Charles staged an ascension of his own balloon before the Parisians assembled during a local celebration at the Champ de Mars. It was a pretty sight to watch the balloon climb, then quickly become lost to the naked eye. The large gathering went wild with excitement. But the balloon cover was not entirely gastight, and so the hydrogen soon escaped. The balloon came down near the village of Gonesse, where the local peasantry accorded it a not too enlightened reception. This monster frightened the farmers, who proceeded to attack it with their agricultural tools. For good measure, they tied the balloon cover to a horse and had it dragged to complete destruction.

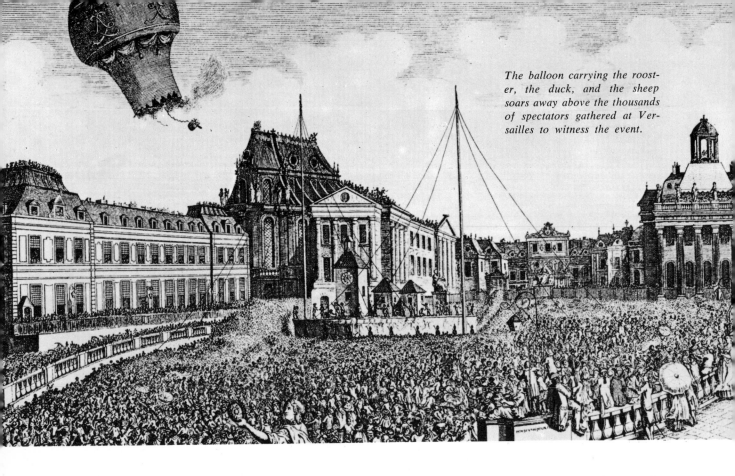

The balloon carrying the rooster, the duck, and the sheep soars away above the thousands of spectators gathered at Versailles to witness the event.

The First Air Passengers:
A Rooster, a Duck,
and a Sheep

As soon as Paris received news of the first balloon ascension in Annonay, the Montgolfier brothers were invited to demonstrate their invention in the French capital. They began at once to build a new, large, and beautifully decorated paper balloon. (This style of hot-air balloon has ever since been called a Montgolfière after its inventors.) The brothers also decided that, though a balloon ascension was a novelty in itself, they would add a special feature to the event: some living creatures would go aloft in the balloon.

It must be remembered that at this time little was known for sure about the conditions prevailing in the "air ocean." Experiments conducted in mountain regions had shown that air density decreased as the altitude increased, but what would happen in a rapidly climbing balloon?

The Montgolfiers selected a rooster, a duck, and a sheep to be the first air passengers on record. The balloon was launched on the occasion of another national festival—September 19, 1783—in Versailles, and the whole court turned out for the event. A basket containing the three animals dangled below the balloon, arousing great interest and curiosity among the huge crowd that was present.

A grate with embers, mounted below the balloon cover, kept the air inside the balloon heated. But this fire soon died out, and only eight minutes after the balloon had been sent up, it descended in the forest of Vancresson.

All the spectators wondered how the animals had fared, and soon a dispatch rider arrived with information: all three had survived. Only the rooster had suffered any injury. One of his wings had been broken, but this damage had been caused by the nervous sheep when the balloon landed, not by any unknown forces in the air.

A Dream Is Fulfilled—Man Travels in the Air!

If animals were able to survive an aerial voyage, so undoubtedly could human beings. Hence, in the spring, the Montgolfier brothers prepared to make man's dream of navigating the air ocean come true. They built the largest and most elaborate balloon they had yet made and decorated it with striking patterns in rococo style. A circular gallery was mounted around the bottom of the big bag, for the balloon pilot and his assistant.

Louis XVI would not let any of his worthy subjects risk their lives, and so decreed that two criminals condemned to death should be the first human beings to go aloft. But two noblemen persuaded the king to change his decision, arguing that criminals did not deserve the glory of being recorded in the annals of human progress as the first air travelers. As a result, that honor belongs to a museum official, Jean François Pilâtre de Rozier, and his companion, the Marquis d'Arlandes. The balloon was to have ascended from Versailles again, but because the throngs there might be uncontrollable, the event was moved to Château de la Muette.

Pilâtre de Rozier made several solo, tied ascensions beforehand. Then the great day for the historic trip was fixed for November 21, 1783. The weather was somewhat windy, but the balloon rose well, to the cheers of the spectators. At last man moved in the air!

This history-making trip lasted only twenty-five minutes, but it was not uneventful. After the balloon had been in the air just a few minutes, large brown spots appeared on the lower part of the cover and small flames began to lick the rim at the mouth of the balloon. Fortunately, Pilâtre de Rozier had provided himself with a large wet sponge for such an emergency. He succeeded in extinguishing the fire, but he also had to douse the embers heating the air inside the balloon, and that resulted in a forced landing.

The largest, handsomest balloon so far, launched from the chateau park of La Muette on November 21, 1783, with the first two human passengers.

The First and Only Balloon Ascension of Professor Charles

Hot-air and gas-filled balloons competed to a certain degree, each type having its devoted advocates.

Professor Charles had been present when the Montgolfier brothers launched their balloon at La Muette. He at once resolved to furnish proof that his kind of balloon could likewise carry passengers. Since he had raised the 10,000 francs his first balloon cost by public subscription, he again sought public support, and within a few days he had raised a like amount.

The new balloon was to carry two passengers, Professor Charles himself and one of the Robert brothers. The hydrogen to fill the balloon was developed in twenty-five barrels, then led to a large one for cleaning and cooling before being fed to the balloon. The date set for the ascension was December 1, 1783.

In the beginning, all went according to plan. The balloon stayed aloft an hour, the longest flight yet made, then came down at Nesle where the Duc de Chartres and an enthusiastic crowd were gathered.

Historians of aeronautics disagree about what happened during the stay of the balloon at Nesle. Some believed, no doubt correctly, that Professor Charles asked Robert to leave the car so that he himself might ascend again, solo. Others think that Robert committed almost the worst of all cardinal sins in ballooning—leaving the car before told to by the pilot. Such a decrease in weight causes the balloon to rise again.

In any case, the Charlière naturally took off again as soon as Robert got out, and in the course of the next

Professor Charles had by now improved his procedure for producing hydrogen, and the balloon filled rapidly.

The ring holding the net at the equator was slightly displaced when the professor and Robert took off.

22

twenty minutes Charles climbed, according to his own estimate, to an altitude of "1,500 fathoms."

Later, he wrote in a report, "When I ascended again, the sun had set already, but it soon rose again for me alone; I was the only lighted object while all the rest of nature was shaded. But then the sun disappeared once more, and thus I had viewed two sunsets in one day. For the next few seconds I could contemplate the ambient air and the steam arising from valleys and rivers. The clouds appeared to ascend from the ground and form layers. Only the moon shone on them."

This air voyage may not have thrilled Professor Charles as much as one would think from his report, for it was the first and last time he ever set foot in a balloon car.

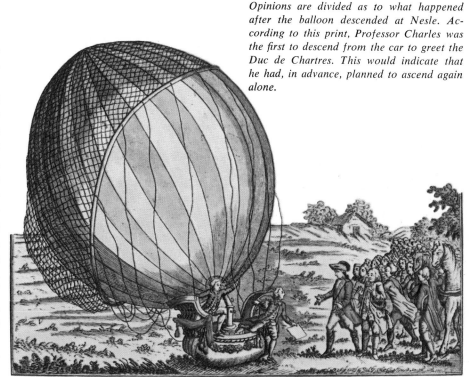

Opinions are divided as to what happened after the balloon descended at Nesle. According to this print, Professor Charles was the first to descend from the car to greet the Duc de Chartres. This would indicate that he had, in advance, planned to ascend again alone.

Here Professor Charles ascends alone from Nesle.   23

What Can the Balloon Accomplish?

America's Benjamin Franklin was one of the spectators who watched Pilâtre de Rozier and the Marquis d'Arlandes take off at La Muette. He was afterward asked what useful future purpose the balloon might serve. His sage reply is reported to have been in the form of a counter-question: "Of what use is a newborn baby?"

It was only natural for people to wonder about the usefulness of future balloon ascensions after the excitement of the first few of them had worn off and they were no longer a novelty. Indeed, what could a balloon accomplish?

The immediate hope was that the balloon would prove to be an efficient means of transportation. However, to attain that goal, any new craft would have to be independent of wind and weather, and controllable by man himself. These characteristics the balloon lacked. The balloon pilot was unable to move about at will—he could go only in the direction the wind blew him, and influence only the climb and descent of the balloon.

In the excitement of the first years of ballooning, the solution was believed to be just around the corner. In 1784 the Academy in Lyon offered a prize for an answer to the question, "How can one steer a balloon?" Almost a hundred suggestions were received, all displaying vivid imagination of a high degree, but—alas—all totally impractical.

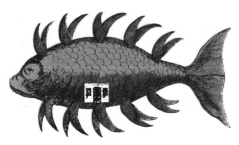

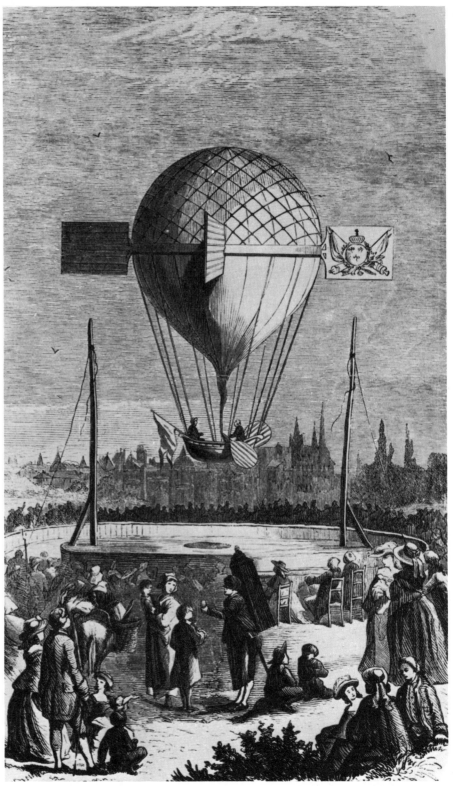

The air was compared to water. One can navigate at sea with a pilot at the helm, so it was reasoned that it must be possible to navigate in the air with a balloon. It was tempting to think that man might similarly paddle or sail through the air—at least during calm weather. Yet such was not the case. At this ascension in Dijon on April 25, 1784, the aeronaut was outfitted with large oars, but they proved useless. Nor were the four rudders effective. The obvious reason was not recognized at the time.

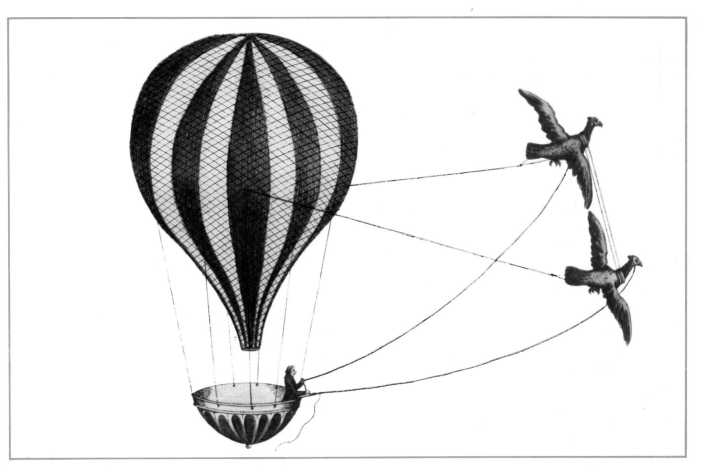

A small book published in Vienna in 1801 presented this idea. It is hard to believe anyone considered it practical. A team of eagles, to be guided like horses, was to provide the propulsion.

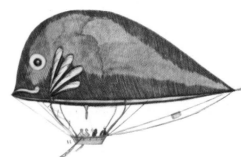

A curious and impractical scheme from 1784. Its best feature was the streamlined fish shape of the balloon.

LEFT: A 1785 drawing suggested the use of sails. Note the gas burner for heating the air in the balloon. In that respect, the scheme was ahead of its day—the modern hot-air balloon is heated this way.

25

Lunardi's first balloon ascension in London on September 15, 1784.

The Balloon Fever Spreads

By the middle of the 1780s, balloon ascensions were being staged at several places in Europe.

It was the French aeronaut Jean-Pierre Blanchard who introduced ballooning in Germany. On October 3, 1785, he ascended at Frankfurt-am-Main; later, he made ascensions in other German cities as well.

An Italian, Vincent Lunardi, attached to his country's embassy in London, made the first balloon ascension from that city on September 15, 1784. Later he made twelve additional ascensions in England. An accident occurred during the last one on September 19, 1786, when a youngster by the name of Ralph Heron was caught by the drag rope of the runaway balloon and lifted from the ground. Unable to hold on to the rope during this involuntary air trip, the boy dropped to his death. (See page 191.) After this fatality, Lunardi made no more balloon ascensions in England.

Son of an Oxford confectioner, James Sadler was the first English-born aeronaut. He made his first ascension in a Montgolfière from his native town on October 7, 1784, but quickly switched to a gas-filled balloon. His two sons followed in their father's footsteps and in turn became popular balloon pilots.

26

Richard Crosbie, the first to make a balloon ascension in Ireland, became an Irish hero. On May 12, 1785, he was to undertake his second ascension, from Palatine Square in Dublin. However, the balloon refused to rise with its load, and so Crosbie got out, greatly disappointing the public. A young officer, Richard McGuire, jumped aboard and threw out all the ballast, whereupon the balloon took off quickly. The spectators gasped with excitement as the balloon headed for the sea. A nobleman, Henry Fitzgerald, hurriedly arranged for a vessel to go to its aid. The balloon descended into the Irish Sea. McGuire is shown being hauled on board the rescue vessel; Lord Fitzgerald is an onlooker in the boat in the background, pointing at the rescue scene. McGuire made a triumphal entry into Dublin, was knighted for his courage, and was received by the Duke of Rutland.

Lunardi in the balloon car with a lady companion, Mrs. Sage. There was a third passenger, George Biggin, not seen in this colored print of the attempted ascension from St. George Field. The load proved too heavy for the lift of the balloon, so Lunardi dismounted and the two others made the ascension alone.

Others have learned by experience that it can be risky to make ascensions from an island country. Here it is a Britisher, Major John Money, who has been downed at sea after an ascension from Norwich in 1785. He too was luckily rescued by a vessel that came to his support. He died in 1817, with the rank of general.

27

The daredevil Jean-Pierre Blanchard, the first to cross the English Channel by air.

An old print shows Blanchard and Dr. Jeffries in their balloon. The oars were of no help at all.

Crossing the English Channel by Air—Triumph and Tragedy

One goal attracted French and English aeronauts more than any other: to be the first to cross the Channel by air. The enterprising and experienced Pilâtre de Rozier keenly desired to win this distinction. In the fall of 1784 he built a balloon of a new type, a combination of ball-shaped Charlière on top and large, tubular, funnel-shaped Montgolfière underneath. Termed a Rozière, it was destined to become a disastrous type, as might have been predicted. Hydrogen is highly explosive when mixed with air, and in the Rozière this dangerous gas was in close proximity to the open fire.

In December 1784, Pilâtre de Rozier took up residence on the French side of the Channel in Boulogne-sur-Mer with his young assistant, P. A. de Romain. Their balloon was completed while they waited for a favorable wind to carry them to England. For a long time the weather was against them.

Meanwhile, the veteran aeronaut Jean-Pierre Blanchard had joined the race to be first across the Channel by air. He wanted to start from Dover on the English coast and had lined up a wealthy American physician to finance his attempt. His relationship with his sponsor was not of the best. The ambitious Blanchard was apparently a bit unscrupulous—he was reluctant to share with Dr. Jeffries the honor of the first aerial crossing of the Channel, and so he took to wearing a concealed belt studded with pieces of lead, in order to convince Jeffries the balloon could not carry him and the pilot as well. Blanchard was found out, however, and the commanding officer at Dover Castle had to arbitrate between the two. Dr. Jeffries sportingly agreed to jump overboard if it turned out that the trip across the Channel could not be completed otherwise.

Blanchard and Jeffries got a head start on Pilâtre de Rozier and de Romain, taking off on a cold and windy day, January 7, 1785. For a while all went well. Then the balloon began to lose altitude. Finally, it almost touched the chilly waters of the English Channel, though one ballast bag after another was thrown overboard. Next, their baggage and every expendable piece of equipment were sacrificed, but to no avail—the balloon would not gain altitude. To relieve it of still more weight, in their despair they even began to undress.

Pilâtre de Rozier, the first air traveler and the first aeronautical fatality.

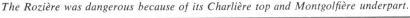
The Rozière was dangerous because of its Charlière top and Montgolfière underpart.

But the French coast was in sight at last—and they managed to reach the beach and land there. (By that time, though, Blanchard had parted with his trousers.) The men were justly rewarded for their efforts. The city of Calais paid them tumultuous homage and made Blanchard an honorary citizen. His balloon was bought for a large sum and displayed in one of the local churches, and a monument was erected to commemorate their achievement.

Pilâtre de Rozier and de Romain naturally were greatly disappointed to have been beaten, but they waited patiently in Boulogne, unwilling to abandon their attempt to be at least the first across the Channel by air from the opposite direction. On June 15, 1785, they took off in their pretty balloon, but the voyage was brief. Strong gusts of wind soon blew them back toward the French coast, and the horrified spectators saw the balloon catch fire and plunge to the ground. Both men were killed.

Pilâtre de Rozier had been the first to make man's age-old dream of traveling in the air come true. He also became the first fatality in the annals of aeronautics.

A woodcut of the plunge of the Rozière with its two occupants.

Spying on the Enemy

During the battle of Fleurus, an officer kept the commanding general, Jourdan, posted on enemy movements by means of messages dropped from an observation balloon.

The first years of ballooning coincided with a bloody chapter in the history of Europe—the wars of Napoleon followed in rapid succession. Quite naturally, his armies considered the military usefulness of the balloon.

It was two French army officers, Nicolas Conté and Captain Jean Coutelle, who proposed employing the balloon as an observation post for spying on enemy lines and movements, since it could provide a wide and unhampered view. The balloon would be held by strong ropes for easy let-out and haul-down. Thus the captive balloon was created.

The so-called welfare committee decreed on April 2, 1794, that an "aeronautical company" be formed, made up of a captain, four noncommissioned officers, and twenty privates.

The first captive balloon was allotted to the Sambre-Meuse army and used initially during the siege of the Charleroi fortress. Later, a balloon was used successfully during the battle of Fleurus, won by the French. On that occasion, reports of enemy movements were put on scraps of paper, which were dropped to the ground weighted with sandbags.

As is so often the case with military innovations, opinions were divided about the value of the balloon section. The military mind is prone to think along conventional lines, but Napoleon was at least interested enough to order Corté to join the campaign against Egypt in 1798 with the most elaborate balloon equipment produced thus far.

In Egypt, Napoleon once more was up against his archenemy England. After his army of 32,000 men had been landed, but before the balloon equipment could be unloaded, Nelson attacked his fleet in Aboukir Bay and partly destroyed it. The balloons were rendered unserviceable. Napoleon never again used balloons in a campaign.

OPPOSITE: *A woodcut (from* Illustrated Family Journal, Copenhagen*) of the engagement at Mannheim in 1794, where the French also used a balloon. Though the Germans claimed to have hit it with gunfire, the balloon stayed aloft. The damage could not have been as bad as shown.*

A Scheme for Invading England by Balloon

When Napoleon planned to invade England, his operational preparations included some vague ideas about employing balloons. However, these ideas never materialized.

It must be admitted that the likelihood of balloons being suited to play an active part in such a venture was extremely slim. To begin with, only a limited number of soldiers could be carried across the Channel, even in the largest balloons. Furthermore, on the day of the invasion, the wind would have to be blowing in a favorable direction. And finally, balloons are pretty vulnerable to gunfire from the ground.

In this artist's conception of the invasion, the balloons are as numerous as the landing craft. There is even a tunnel below the Channel to serve as a further aid in the operation.

Whoever imagined this balloon invasion near Dover must have considered the combined hot-air and gas balloon the most efficient type, and must also have remained undiscouraged by the sad end of Pilâtre de Rozier and Romain's attempt to cross the Channel in a Rozière. No doubt he figured that hydrogen would provide maximum lift and carrying capacity, and "the hot-air section" would both add a boost and provide the means of a rapid descent if the situation called for one. Still, he had Utopian faith to believe that so much cavalry and war equipment could be carried by balloons.

OPPOSITE: An artist's idea of a French observation balloon in 1795. The pastoral scene looks almost as if the soldiers are pursuing a peaceful sport.

Early American and English Balloon Pilots

It was the enterprising Blanchard who, on January 9, 1793, made the first balloon ascension in the United States. The political climate in Europe had become too hot for his comfort—for a time he had been imprisoned in a fortress on account of the views he expressed. So, after forty-four European balloon ascensions, Blanchard embarked on the Philadelphia-bound vessel *Ceres* out of Hamburg on September 30, 1792, and on December 9 disembarked at his destination with his balloon and "4200 weight of vitriolic acid, enough for one ascension by him alone." During his extended stay in the national capital of the newly founded United States of America, the city directory for Philadelphia bore this entry for 9 North Eighth Street: Blanchard, the celebrated aeronaut.

Before his ascension, Blanchard received several requests from people wishing to accompany him as passengers. The aeronaut informed the press that if he accepted a passenger, an additional supply of vitriolic acid must be bought locally to produce the extra lift required, and it would cost at least $300.

No wonder that time and again professional aeronauts of the early days found their ascensions expensive and unprofitable affairs. This remained the situation right down through the exhibition flights of the early airplanes, after the novelty of seeing them in the air and the willingness to pay handsomely for it wore off. There was no circumventing the fact that spectators outside the grounds could witness what was going on just as well as those willing to pay for doing so. And Blanchard's first air voyage in America was no exception. His expenses amounted to $1,500, which he hoped to recover by advance sales of $5 and $2 tickets, but the gate receipts amounted to only $405. Those who had a guilty conscience about viewing the impressive sight for free contributed another $263 afterward.

Often, balloon pilots performing publicly did not make ends meet, and later, in delicate terms, would appeal to the nobler instincts of the crowds. An advertisement inserted in a local newspaper by the English aeronaut Graham was typical. He explained his deficit on that occasion, in the hope of recovering the money—or most of it. Only once have we found records of a different nature—when "Professor Étienne Robertson wrote of his first balloon ascension in Denmark:

"There were such crowds pressing to enter the admission gates that I decided to open them early to relieve the pressure in the adjoining streets. Thereby I could have sacrificed a large part of my intake, but I did not hesitate for one moment. What no doubt will surprise many, and gained my sincere admiration, was that I did not become the loser from this action. As the hordes of humanity were forced through the gates they voluntarily produced their admission money—they did not want to enter free. What a difference in behavior between the pure conscience of the common people and the aristocratic indifference of the nobility in Moscow. There, without contributing anything from their own purses, these noblemen sat comfortably in their carriages and enjoyed a spectacle that is always pretty costly." (Robertson later reported that he took in 20,000 francs in Copenhagen.)

To return to Blanchard and his only balloon ascension in the New World: it was of forty-six minutes' duration, and a distance of fifteen miles had been covered when he landed at Woodbury, New Jersey. Washington witnessed the takeoff and handed the pilot a passport. Blanchard was back in Philadelphia the same afternoon to pay his respects to the President of the United States.

Aeronautics history has, like that of other fields, a way of repeating itself. Developments in the English-speaking parts of the Old and New Worlds have run along strikingly similar lines.

In the United States two aeronauts stood out above the others during the nineteenth century: John Wise and Samuel King; in England, Henry Coxwell and Charles Green were outstanding. Wise and Coxwell both wrote books about ballooning that went into two editions; King and Green made record trips and valuable contributions to ballooning techniques.

On July 19, 1821, at a balloon ascension in London, Green was the first to use ordinary illuminating gas for filling the balloon bag, thereby lowering the expense and making ballooning more popular. His introduction of the trailing rope made landings easier and safer. In 1838, Wise invented another safety device, the rip flap for fast deflation. Twice he voluntarily emptied his balloon in midair by keeping his top valve constantly open, to demonstrate that the balloon cover would then press against the top part of the balloon net and act as a parachute, thus permitting a safe descent if the balloon tore accidentally or burst during a trip.

Wise made 462 balloon ascensions, drowning in Lake Michigan on the last one. King lived to the ripe age of over eighty. Like Coxwell and other great

Greenwich, 11th June, 1825.

LOSS

OF

Mr. GRAHAM,

THE AERONAUT.

From the Statement beneath, it will be perceived that the above named Gentleman, in affording Amusement and Gratification to the Inhabitants of Greenwich and its vicinity, by his Ascent on Monday last, and thereby in some degree benefiting the Town, has Sustained a

Loss of £50.11s.2D.

and it having been Suggested to him by several Gentlemen of the place, that provided the same was made known and accompanied by an appeal to the well known liberallity of the Public here, they were convinced it would have the effect of at least alleviating, if not altogether clearing him of so great a Loss. He therefore upon these conditions respectfully informs the Public, that Subscriptions for that purpose will be received at Mr. COLES, Bookseller London Street, Greenwich, and at the BAR OF THE MITRE TAVERN.

EXPENDITURE.	RECEIPT.
£. 91 : 12 : 2	£. 41 : 1 : 0

Printed by J. COLE, London Street, Greenwich.

From the Erik Hildesheim Aeronautica Collections

balloonists, he found it difficult to recognize and reconcile himself to the ultimate superiority of heavier-than-air craft. Coxwell made his first balloon ascension in 1844. He remained an active pilot for forty-one years, making more than 1,000 balloon trips.

America had its own balloon dynasty—the Allens, a father and his sons. England, too, had a dynasty, the Spencers—brothers, sisters, children, and a brother-in-law, Augustus Gaudron, who ascended in both balloons and small dirigibles, and made parachute descents in many parts of the world between 1889 and 1914. In parachuting, they became competitors of Thomas S. Baldwin, America's "Uncle Tom of the Air," who began as a tightrope performer, then took up parachuting at home and abroad. He was the first to provide an air vent in the top of the parachute to arrest its dangerous oscillations during descent. He also began the practice of charging $1.00 per foot of altitude for his jumps.

Uncle Tom's career spanned the whole range of aeronautical developments. He built the first U.S. Army airship on contract; then, at an advanced age, he began the manufacture of his "Red Devil" airplane on the lines of the early Curtiss pusher type. When Baldwin grew stout, he gave up piloting his own planes. He was a lovable character, popular with everyone, but he lost his cheerful disposition in his last years. After his death it was discovered that one of his internal organs had shrunk and might have been responsible for his change of spirit. This physical change, it was presumed, might have been an aftereffect of so many parachute jumps from high altitudes.

In England there were the Short brothers, who began as balloon manufacturers, then took up airplane production. Over the years they specialized in seaplanes and flying boats, turning out some outstanding types.

On April 13, 1844, the *New York Sun* published a long report from Norfolk, Virginia, about the landing of the balloon "Victoria" at Charleston, South Carolina, with nine passengers, after an aerial crossing of the Atlantic. The pilot Monckmason, along with Robert Hollond, M.P., had participated in an extended balloon trip made by Green from England to Weilburg in Nassau, Germany. So it was easy to guess what inspired the author of this news report, Edgar Allan Poe. At first rival papers were envious of the scoop achieved by the *Sun*. Before long, the *Sun* and its readers became a laughingstock for having been taken in so completely.

Once French balloon pilots had gone aloft astride horses, New World aeronauts had to go them one better. When Morat ascended with a passenger from New Orleans on February 8, 1858, the two were mounted on alligators, but it is not reported whether either the men or the beasts enjoyed this experience. And when "Professor" Wilson made a hot-air balloon ascension from the Tuscumbia, Alabama, fairground accompanied by "a beautiful young lady," a regional newspaper commented: "By and by, the ladies will be able to ascend simply by filling their crinolines with smoke—that is all they lack of being angels."

The well-known English aeronaut, Richard Wells, came to America and, on one occasion at New Orleans, filled his balloon with vaporized alcohol. The vapor condensed as soon as the balloon gained some altitude, and a precipitous descent ensued. One spectator was trampled in the crowd that had gathered, and the owner of the landing place sued the city for $500 damages to his porch and flower gardens. Wells switched to a Montgolfière for his next ascent, but to no avail—his landing was again hazardous.

SIC ITUR AD ASTRA

the first
January
delphia
de by
nchard.

45ᵉ ascension et la premiere
faite en Amerique Le 9 Jan-
vier 1793 a Philadelphie 39
56′ Latitude N. par.
M. J. P. Blanchard.

JOURNAL

OF MY

FORTY-FIFTH

ASCENSION,

BEING THE FIRST PERFORMED IN

A M E R I C A,

ON THE NINTH OF JANUARY, 1793.

Æthereum tranabit iter, quo numine BLANCHARD?

Impavidus, sortem non timet Icariam.

PHILADELPHIA:

PRINTED BY CHARLES CIST, No. 104. NORTH

SECOND-STREET, M,DCC,XCIII.

"Professor" Robertson, Magician and Aeronaut

Many early professional balloon pilots tried to lend prestige to their activities by adopting the title "professor." One of the most colorful of these was "Professor" Étienne Gaspard Robertson. He was born in Liège, Belgium, but at an early age settled in Paris, where he became famous for his "ghost performances."

Robertson became equally famed as a balloon pilot. He ascended in Russia, Austria, and Spain, and in 1806 was the first to go aloft in Sweden and Denmark. In the summer of 1803 he made the first "scientific" balloon trip, accompanied by a fellow aeronaut, Lhoest. Their extravagant claims about the height they had reached and their observations gave rise to doubts of their veracity, and inspired scientists of established reputation to make ascensions to learn the altitude human beings could reach and withstand.

An excerpt from Robertson's report of this balloon trip reads: "We continued to climb as long as our health would stand it. . . . At that altitude, and in spite of the condition we then were in, I tried to read the Volta column and to observe the flight of birds and other happenings as long as possible . . . But my head had become so swollen that I no longer could wear my cap. When blood began to trickle from my eyes, I let the balloon descend. The farmers on the ground apparently were frightened by the sight of my balloon, and since I had forgotten to make a very important experiment, I let the balloon climb once more." Robertson claimed that in the higher regions he reached there was no atmospheric air, only fumes, and that the earth's magnetism had lost part of its strength. No wonder scientists termed the "professor" a bragging liar.

Robertson's sons, Eugène and Dimitri, became skilled balloon performers, too. They made ascensions in France, Portugal, the United States,

"Professor" Robertson knew how to entertain the public. Here he ascends with a parachute attached to the balloon, with which he will shortly jump.

The First Scientific Balloon Ascension

and Cuba in 1826 and 1827, and in Mexico in 1835, where Eugène died two years later. Dimitri made ascensions in Russia, then went to Calcutta for others, where he died in 1836.

The French Academy of Science entered the violent controversy about "Professor" Roberston's strange observations, and as a result it was decided to let two reputable physicists, Joseph Gay-Lussac and Jean Baptiste Biot, undertake the first truly scientific balloon ascension. They ascended from Paris on August 24, 1804, equipped with numerous instruments wherewith to check Robertson's claims. Also carried in the balloon were a bird, frogs, and various insects.

This balloon ascension served mainly to disprove at least part of Robertson's "discoveries." The electrical and magnetic deflections showed normal readings. When released, the bird flapped its wings furiously in becoming airborne, but later investigations established the fact that pigeons do experience difficulties in sustaining themselves at great altitudes.

Gay-Lussac and Biot also had with them a glass vacuum bottle, which they filled with air at high altitude. Thus they verified the nonexistence of the "fumes" reported by Robertson.

Madame Blanchard Plunges to Her Death

The daredevil Jean-Pierre Blanchard lost his life in a balloon accident in 1809, but his widow, Madéleine-Sophie Blanchard, carried on the family tradition. Even while her husband was still alive, she was one of the most popular "heroes" of the air at that time. Though she was reported to be terrified of traveling in a horse-drawn carriage, she was fearless in the air.

On June 24, 1810, a balloon ascension from the Champ de Mars in Paris formed part of the celebration in honor of the marriage of Napoleon to Marie-Louise of Austria. Madame Blanchard was the natural choice as the balloon pilot on that occasion.

Madame Blanchard specialized in setting off fireworks during her ascensions, and this practice was to prove her undoing when indulged in once too often. Her luck ran out on a balloon ascension from Paris on July 7, 1819. A contemporary report describes what happened:

"A golden shower streams in currents from the balloon car. Then, by parachute, she drops a bomb emitting a silver rain. Still another shower of fire sparks emerges from the car. Excited, the crowd applauds—they have not yet realized Madame's car has caught fire. She knows what has happened, however, but does not lose her head. Quickly she drops some ballast as the balloon rapidly sinks. Now the fire is almost arrested, and it looks as if Madame Blanchard will land safely. Suddenly a gust of wind catches the car, making it crash into the roof of a house in Rue de Provence. Madame falls to the street, dead of a broken neck."

M. S. BLANCHARD célèbre aéronaute

Madame Blanchard was a trim lady, small of stature but great in courage when it came to handling fireworks in a hydrogen-filled balloon.

BELOW: *Madame Blanchard plunges from her somewhat impractically shaped balloon car to her death.*

40

Madame Blanchard's ascension from the Champ de Mars during the wedding festivities of Napoleon and Marie-Louise.

41

Ballooning Becomes a Favorite Public Entertainment

Balloon ascensions began as a form of public entertainment, and so they remained for many years except for the ascensions undertaken to make scientific observations. This was true both in Europe and America—these ascensions invariably were such impressive sights that they attracted more attention than any other spectacle.

The early balloon developments occurred in France. While they were taking place, of course, bloody and historic events also marked these revolutionary times. But it suited the men responsible for the new social order to amuse the crowds simultaneously with huge balloon displays.

A considerable number of the pilots who participated in these activities tried to outdo one another in thinking of new stunts to include. The aeronaut André Jacques Garnerin was the first to add a thrill to his balloon trips by descending with a parachute. In 1798 another daredevil, Pierre Tétu-Brissy, ascended in an oblong Charlière while mounted on a horse standing on a rectangular platform below. The horse enjoyed the performance less than the attending public. The be-kind-to-animals people began to protest against this kind of air display.

One of the most beautiful balloon prints available, this one shows a Montgolfière ascension from the Tivoli Gardens in Paris in 1800. The spectators are beautifully garbed, and the whole scene breathes a relaxed, almost poetic atmosphere contrasting sharply with the violent happenings of the time. The well-dressed audience does not reflect the frugality called for by the Revolutionary edict. However, even Robespierre himself sometimes abandoned his somber clothes. When elected president of the Convention, he wore a purple velvet jacket, yellow breeches with a tricolor scarf around the waist, silk stockings, a powdered wig, and a plumed hat.

Henry Monnier's drawing, "The Happy Match." After about 1820, women's fashions turned away from the Empire style—there had been enough imitation of ancient styles. A different fashion now came into vogue, clearly showing the influence of the balloon. Bulgy skirts looked as if they covered an inflated balloon, and sleeves resembled puffy balloons.

Here, one of the Poitevin family of balloonists goes aloft on horseback, around 1850.

LEFT: *Tétu-Brissy's ascension mounted on a nervous horse.*

RIGHT: *The French announcement of the Tétu-Brissy ascension.*

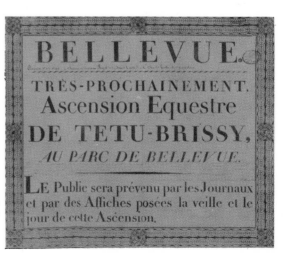

BELLEVUE.

TRÈS-PROCHAINEMENT,
Ascension Equestre
DE TETU-BRISSY,
AU PARC DE BELLEVUE.

LE Public sera prévenu par les Journaux et par des Affiches posées la veille et le jour de cette Ascension.

Tardini's Tragic End

The poster on this page shows how hydrogen for the early balloons was produced in numerous barrels by passing sulfuric acid over iron filings. The gas was fed to a central pipe, then into the balloon bag.

This particular poster advertised the Italian Tardini's third and, in fact, last ascension from Copenhagen, for he suffered the same fate experienced by so many other aeronauts who came to grief over the water: he jumped overboard to save the lives of his two passengers, his son and a woman companion, who were rescued in shallow water.

Evidence of the attraction of balloon ascensions is given by the last line of the poster: "His Majesty, the King, will honor this performance by his most gracious presence."

Joseph Giuseppe Tardini, a luckless aeronaut.

Still
Going
Strong

In contrast to the illustration on the opposite page, the picture at the right shows a present-day balloon ascension from Tivoli Gardens in Copenhagen. Such events still attract large crowds, but nowadays the balloons are generally filled with cooking gas or, if of the hot-air type, the gas burner is bottle fed.

One thing remains unchanged: the professional pilot is quite likely to climb up onto the edge of the car to show his bravery and to wave to the admiring crowds on the ground. In this picture, the pilot is the veteran Swiss aeronaut Eduard Spelterini, well known for his crossings of the Alps by balloon and for the fine aerial photographs he has taken all over the world.

Large-sized Balloons

RIGHT: *At the turn of the nineteenth century it was thought the balloon would become the popular travel vehicle of the future, even cause traffic congestion in the air. An English artist imagined balloon stands in the streets, from which rapid ascensions might be made. The sign-covered buildings in the background rival Times Square and Piccadilly Circus.*

BELOW: *The balloon rage took many forms. In this amusement park, youngsters are catered to with miniature balloons like the large ones provided for grown-ups.*

Artist's conception of the first balloon launching from the citadel at Copenhagen. In actuality, the balloon failed to rise. The means of propulsion was purely a product of the artist's imagination.

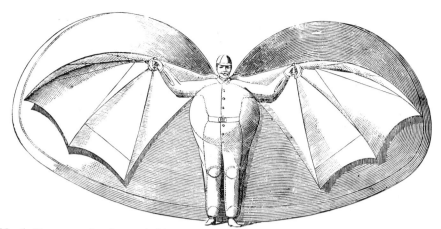

North Star *magazine featured this picture of "the flying man" in 1886. The caption read: "The newest flying apparatus has been invented by an Austrian, Baron von Wechmar. Based upon a sensible combination of the inherent advantages of the balloon and the wing-flapping vehicle, the outfit consists of a flat balloon encompassing the body of the operator, plus a set of large bat wings. The operator also wears protective air pads on breast and knees, to cushion him should he crash." "Safety first" was obviously a popular slogan even then.*

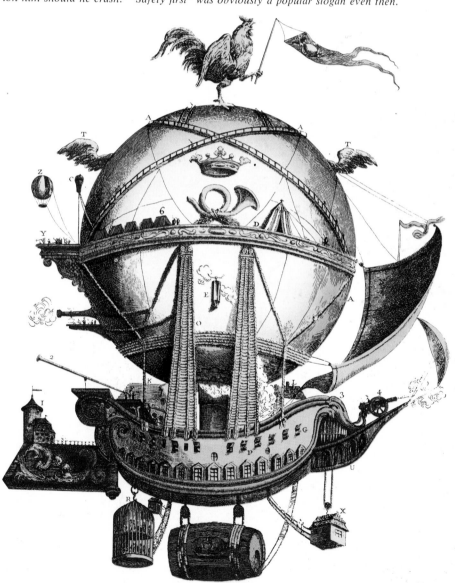

In 1803, "Professor" Robertson proposed this "airship," named "Minerva," for an expedition by sixty outstanding scientists to far corners of the world. He described the craft and his aims in great detail. Perhaps he wanted his statements to be taken seriously, but since he enjoyed indulging in magic tricks, one suspects him of a bit of leg-pulling.

The ship was to have splendid rooms for conferences and games, studios for music and study, even a church. The women members of the expedition would have their own pavilion, far removed from the others, lest they distract the men from serious work. There would be guns for firing salutes, spare balloons for side trips to the ground, a huge barrel of German beer to serve as both refreshment and expendable ballast—but why go on?

47

Large-sized Balloons

By the middle of the nineteenth century, some very large balloons had been built, mostly in France. The largest ones had a cabin equal to a small cottage in size, with woven walls, and could accommodate a considerable number of passengers. Gaston Tissandier was one of the most skilled French balloon pilots. In the large balloon "North Pole," built to his order, he made some interesting ascensions. Like others, he took advantage of the fact that the wind often blows in different directions at different altitudes. He once left the French coast and when well out over the English Channel found another air current that returned his balloon to the Continent, thus demonstrating that balloons are in a sense dirigible to a slight degree. Tissandier made scientific observations as well, and experimented with various types of thermometers, including rotary types, which gave more accurate readings of air temperature than previously possible. He discovered that the temperature inside a balloon might easily be as high as 23° C. though the outside air might produce a below-freezing reading of minus 5° C.

Large balloons called for large anchors. This one was designed by von Hervé.

ABOVE: *Tissandier brings the "North Pole" back to the French coast.*

LEFT: *Tissandier and his companions in the large basket of the "North Pole."*

Filling large balloons required many thousands of cubic feet of hydrogen, and also many barrels in which to produce and purify it.

A close-up of the car of Eugène Godard's balloon "The Eagle," which reportedly made ascensions between 1864 and 1866. This balloon, apparently a Montgolfière, was almost 500,000 cubic feet in capacity.

"Captain" Godard stands on the railing. The passengers are dressed in the height of fashion for that period. The figure directly below "The Eagle" looks for all the world like Charles Dickens.

49

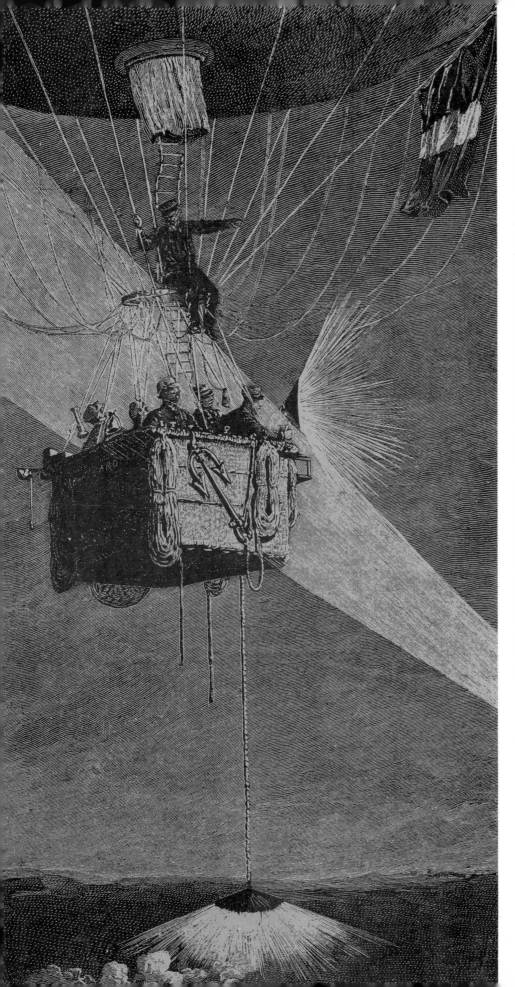

Aeronauts generally told the altitude of the balloon by barometric readings. In the late 1890s a French inventor believed he had developed something better for that purpose. His method consisted of a camera mounted below the balloon basket in such a way that it could both shoot the landscape below and take a picture of the barometer hanging on one of the net lines. Then, when (1) the focus distance had been determined, (2) the distance between two points in the landscape had been determined, and (3) this distance was compared with another on the photograph, the altitude could be calculated.

The method was useless on cloudy days, and in any case the altitude of the balloon at a given moment could not be calculated until it had landed and the pictures were developed.

Above is a photograph of a landscape with a barometer superimposed.

TOP, OPPOSITE: *The worshiped Nadar. (Woodcut by A. Grevin, about 1870.)*
RIGHT: *Sarah Bernhardt photographed by Nadar in 1859.*

One of the large French balloons, "Figaro," on military maneuvers. Here, as it is caught by a searchlight from the Eiffel Tower, an officer signals back to Paris.

The World's First Aerial Photographer

Gaspard Félix Tornachon, better known as Félix Nadar, the most renowned photographer of his time in Paris, also experimented with large balloons. In his studio on the Boulevard des Capucines, he photographed the great authors and artists of the day—Manet, Corot, Dumas, Baudelaire, George Sand, Jules Verne, Delacroix, Sarah Bernhardt, Daumier, Doré, Berlioz, Wagner, and many others. Nadar was a first-rate artist with the camera, but in discussions as to whether photography was a proper art, he argued that it would never supersede painting or decrease the stature of a real work of art.

In a way, Nadar was the world's first aerial photographer. On October 23, 1858, he had taken out a patent on a "system of aerostatic photography" with the object of developing topographical photo maps. ("Aerostatic machines" was the term originally applied to balloons.) But the first successful photographs taken from the air were those made of Boston by a photographer named Black who, on April 18, 1861, went aloft with the American aeronaut King, in his captive balloon. Nadar himself took some good aerial shots of a section of Paris in 1868 from Henri Giffard's captive balloon, but previous to that, aerial photographs for strategic purposes had already been taken during the American Civil War by Thaddeus Lowe of the Union Armies opposite Richmond, Virginia.

One of many photographs of Paris taken from the air by Nadar in the 1860s.

The Dramatic Voyage of "The Giant"

Nadar's "Giant" was indeed large—131 feet tall, with a capacity of more than 280,000 cubic feet. The balloon car ("balloon house" would be a more appropriate term) was 16 feet high and outfitted with a small printing press and a photographic studio. Nadar had a sense of the dramatic and knew the value of advertising—his printing press turned out a handbill in six languages with this request: "The finder hereof is requested to hand this circular to the city editor of the nearest newspaper, as the whole world most anxiously awaits word of the fate of 'The Giant Balloon.'"

These handbills almost had to be called into service on the second ascension of the balloon on October 18, 1863. The Godard brothers were the pilots on that occasion, and were accompanied by Nadar and his wife as well as several passengers. The following is a report of their exciting trip:

"This air voyage began at dusk and was most pleasant for the first sixteen hours. Early next morning we passed the German city of Hannover and prepared to land. Godard ordered the valve opened to let out gas, and the ballast bags were lined up in easy reach, so that they could be dropped at the proper moment to reduce the shock when we hit the ground. We were horrified when the balloon descended much faster than calculated. Godard just had time to instruct everybody to hold on to anything suitable that could be grasped, but before his orders could be obeyed the car hit the ground violently and we were thrown helter-skelter. A storm had sprung up, and it pulled us along at a terrific pace. Every other instant the car collided with something, and then the balloon would make a giant bounce before hitting the ground again. This performance lasted a half hour. We did not get smashed ourselves, but crushed everything standing in our path. When we neared some railroad tracks, we saw a train come racing along and we shouted in fright. The train fortunately stopped and we passed safely by after knocking down the telegraph poles. Several passengers were injured by the time the balloon car came to rest."

LEFT: *"The Giant" (in name and fact) being transported to the Champ de Mars in Paris, prior to its ascension.* (Illustrated News, *1863.*)

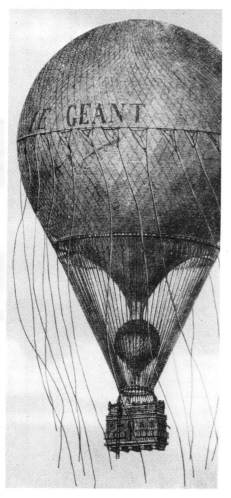

"The Giant" in the air.

The balloon cabin knocked down even large trees while it was being dragged rapidly along on the ground after the landing. The train is seen in the background.

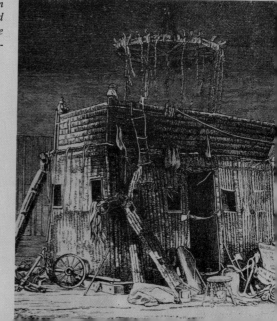

The balloon cabin, after it was knocked about in the dramatic landing.

In 1847 the professional English aeronaut Richard Gypson had a trying experience when his balloon was torn during an ascension in stormy weather. He survived to endorse the truth of the words: "All's well that ends well." The balloon cover pressed against the top part of the net and acted as a parachute.

This illustration, from the introduction to the chapter on balloons in the German edition of Book of Inventions, dates from the middle 1870s. It shows the dangers the general public associated with ballooning.

Balloon pilots used to dread landings in trees because their balloons were likely to be torn to shreds. In 1839 the experienced American pilot John Wise invented the so-called rip flap that, when pulled while landing, emptied the balloon faster than the gas would escape by opening the valve. This prevented the balloon from being dragged on the ground for a long distance when landing in a high wind.

No More Risk than Going Fishing?

After the balloon pilot Thomas Harris ascended in London in 1824, he discovered that the gas valve was stuck and the hydrogen rapidly escaping through the opening. The resulting descent was dangerously abrupt. Harris jumped out to save his woman companion, as other pilots have done in similar situations. She fainted on the ground, but recovered. Thomas Harris was killed.

A balloon pilot once remarked that ballooning was as safe as going fishing. His statement requires certain reservations. Countless—in fact, the great majority of—balloon ascensions are completed without the participants being harmed or exposed to great danger. However, many accidents have occurred, and ballooning cannot be considered a completely safe sport.

Balloonists face several hazards: the gas may escape while they are aloft; the balloon may hit a high building or tall tree; the landing may be rough if the pilot cannot locate suitable terrain; and so on.

Another balloon pilot commented: "Every balloon descent must be considered an emergency landing, though most times the pilot is master of the situation."

Balloons in the Civil War

Students of the War Between the States can always learn much from it, as many technical innovations that were introduced at that time foreshadowed later developments. Thus, we come across several air "firsts" that are not developments of World Wars I and II, as one might suspect, but of America's great civil conflict.

A young German officer with an alert and versatile mind, Count Ferdinand von Zeppelin, was one of those who realized that there was much to be learned in this New World theater of war, and he made a trip to the United States to study it. He witnessed some of Professor Thaddeus Lowe's balloon ascensions on the Union side, though he did not participate in any of them. Zeppelin's interest in aeronautics was increased when he went aloft in a tethered balloon at Minneapolis in the course of an exploration trip along the Mississippi River.

The Prussians were at that time predominant in military matters, but this officer from one of the southern German states retired from his military career when he was passed over for promotion some time later. Not until then did he attempt to act on his idea for a large, rigid airship and, with true Teutonic stubbornness, see it through.

Both the Confederate and Union armies used balloons for making observations. The Confederate States to a great extent lacked the facilities of the North, but they often made up for their deficiencies by their ingenuity. The first Confederate balloons were varnished cotton bags—Montgolfières tethered with a single rope, and thus pretty unstable. The air, heated by an ample supply of pine knots and turpentine, soon cooled off, and at best did not provide too much lift. The rope, half a mile in length, had one end tied to a tree, then was passed around a windlass and attached to the balloon net. To hasten the haul-down through the danger zone (above the protection of trees or from altitudes within the range of gunfire), a team of six artillery horses would be hitched to the windlass and sent galloping down a nearby road.

This novel piece of military equipment always attracted much attention, and interested onlookers frequently hampered its operation. One day a spectator got caught in the windlass, and his companion cut the rope with an ax to save his limb. It released not only him, but the balloon as well, which drifted across the enemy lines. Then, by good fortune, a change in wind direction drove the balloon back to its own side, though not to complete safety, for friend and foe alike fired indiscriminately at it. Similar treatment was the lot of some aircraft during both world wars.

Nor are blackouts a development of modern warfare. The adjutant of Confederate General Pierre G. T. Beauregard on September 2, 1861, issued the following instructions: "The general of this Army Corps wishes every precaution taken to prevent the enemy from discovering by balloons or other means the numbers of our advanced commands or outposts. No lights should be kept at night except where absolutely necessary, and then under such screens as may conceal the lights from observation. Further, tents, if used, ought to be pitched under the cover of woods and sheltered in all cases as far as possible from accurate computation."

General Beauregard made use of more active camouflage to deceive the opposing aerial observers. In December 1861, he wrote to Major General James Longstreet: ". . . it may become suddenly important to prevent the enemy's balloon observations from discovering whether or not we have guns in our batteries, or more properly to let them believe that we have, you will have at once the position of each gun protected from aerial vision by a shed of leaves and brushwood, elevated six feet from the ground or the height of the crest, putting in each embrasure a piece of wood of the proper size (blackened) to represent a gun. Endeavor to have this done as soon as possible." These crude make-believe cannon became known as "Quaker Guns." General Beauregard also instructed the troops under his command to build fake camp and picket fires to confuse the enemy still more—all of which is exactly the sort of thing the English did in the Battle of Britain to throw off the aim of German bombers and make them waste their bomb loads on fake targets.

The Confederates later had two silk balloons. The first one was constructed by Captain Langdon Cheves, who fell in the naval bombardment of Charleston. According to some reports, he bought the bolts of silk for making his balloon from a local merchant. The balloon was built at the Chatham Armory in Savannah, filled with gas from the Upper Gas Works in Richmond, and towed by a locomotive on the York River Rail Road to its ascension point. It was under the command of Major E. P. Alexander, who recounted in his book *Military Memoirs of a Confederate*: ". . . I was placed in charge of a balloon which had been manufactured in Savannah by Dr. Edward [wrong first name] Cheves and sent to General Lee for use in reconnoitering the enemy lines. It was made from silk of many patterns varnished with gutta-percha car springs dissolved in naphtha, and inflated at the Richmond Gas Works with ordinary city gas."

General James Longstreet wrote, in "Our March Against Pope," from *Battles and Leaders of the Civil War*: "The Federals had been using balloons in examining our positions, and we watched with envious eyes their beautiful observations as they floated high in the air well out of the range of our guns. While we were longing for the balloons that poverty denied us, a genius arose for the occasion and suggested that we send out and gather together all the silk dresses in the Confederacy and make a balloon. It was done, and we soon had a great patchwork ship which was ready for use in the Seven Days' Campaign."

The patriotic sacrifice of their finery by the ladies of the South has been termed "a romantic tale," but the patched appearance of the fabric of at least one of the two Confederate gas balloons seems to bear out the silk-dress story. A letter in the collection of the Savannah Historical Society from a lady at 1015 H Street in Washington, D.C., also appears to provide corroboration: "Miss Cunningham:—It affords me pleasure to share with you as a lady of the 'Palmetto State' the enclosed piece of a balloon made of the silk dresses and oiled by the ladies of South Carolina (Charleston I think) and presented to the Confederate Army for inspection purposes during the late struggle for independance [sic]. It was not captured, but during a high wind came over into the Union lines and was brought to the U.S. Patent Office as a trophy of the War, and there cut up and distributed. It was much torn and useless. I then and there saw the balloon and obtained quite a piece of it. This was I think in 1863. With esteem, believe me, Most truly yrs. Maria S. Thomson."

The translator of this volume possesses a piece of Confederate balloon fabric that has the same patterns as other pieces owned by various institutions. It was given to him by the son of Professor Lowe, mounted in a brief biography of Lowe that the son had prepared. The professor reported obtaining a good sample of this Confederate balloon.

A Union balloon being inflated by means of a portable hydrogen generator, under the supervision of Professor Lowe. The Confederates lacked this efficient means of filling a balloon.

The second Confederate gas balloon was built by, and in charge of, Captain Charles Cevor, who as a civilian balloon pilot had made ascensions in the South just prior to the outbreak of the war. It was filled at the Charleston city gasworks and operated on the James River from the wooden, armed "propeller" (i.e., tugboat) *Teaser,* until captured when this Confederate vessel ran aground and encountered the Union ironclad *Monitor* and her escort, the U.S.S. *Maratanza.* Thus, naval aeronautics likewise originated in the Civil War.

The Union forces also used ships for some of their balloon operations, even introducing the first primitive aircraft carrier. This was the wooden platform vessel *G. W. Parke Custis,* from which Professor Lowe's balloon ascended on the Potomac River. And John La Mountain's observation balloon was stationed on board the vessel *Fanny.*

Union balloon activities were on a more elaborate scale than those on the Confederate side. Professor Thaddeus Lowe was the driving force in this field. In addition to La Mountain, other American balloonists of the time who offered their services and were accepted were the brothers James and Ezra Allen, Steiner, and John Wise.

Lowe experienced great difficulties in gaining acceptance and getting started. First he demonstrated in Washington, D.C., that after ascending in his tethered balloon he could transmit his observations to the ground by telegraph wire. But it required a request from Lincoln written on the President's calling card to obtain an interview with the commanding general for Lowe.

Placed in charge of the Union balloons, Professor Lowe made valuable aerial observations himself. However, many officers remained indifferent to the importance of balloons. Rivalry and jealousy also prevailed among the aeronauts themselves and, disgusted with red-tape interference, Lowe resigned before the Civil War was over. His greatest contribution to the development of the military balloon was the efficient, transportable hydrogen-producing unit he built. Three of them were captured by the Confederates, who were unable to utilize them because they lacked the necessary chemicals.

The pay scale for Professor Lowe's services as a military aeronaut was $10 per day, whereas Cevor, his Confederate opposite number, was paid $140 per month and his civilian assistant received $100 a month.

An Air Travel Sketch from 1852

A famous author gives his imagination free rein and foretells seeing Europe by air during a short vacation.

Throughout his life, Hans Christian Andersen, the Danish author of fairy tales, strove for recognition, and he cherished fame when he had won it. Andersen displayed remarkable vision in one piece he wrote. It was published on January 26, 1852, in the Copenhagen paper *Native Country*. Only its title, "Across the Ocean on Wings of Steam," proved erroneous. His predictions read remarkably like present-day travel-bureau literature. For example, he began: "Yes, a thousand years from now they will be flying across the oceans on wings." But even his lively imagination fell short in the matter of time—his prediction came true less than a century later. In fact, his daring had its limits—after all, he was no science fiction writer prophesying jet aircraft and the atomic age.

It is most unlikely that Andersen's fairly obvious little sketch about the future ever came to the attention of Jules Verne, the renowned French creator of many imaginative tales. Yet it is a strange coincidence that the French writer later did produce a famous balloon story, *Around the World in Eighty Days,* and in it also fell far short of what Mr. Everyman would soon be capable of accomplishing. Curiously, Hans Andersen ended his piece about travel in the future with the phrase, "Europe seen in eight days."

"Yes, a thousand years from now they will be flying across the oceans on wings of steam! The young Americans will visit old Europe just as we in our day pay our respect to the decaying fame of southern Asia.

"They will turn up a thousand years from now!

"The Thames, the Danube, and the Rhine just keep rolling. Mont Blanc still will be there with its snow cap. The Northern Lights will continue to flicker across the sky of the countries of the North, yet one generation after the other will have turned to dust, including many who enjoyed a fleeting renown in their day. They are no different from the wealthy Corn Exchange operator resting in the mound on which we now stand. The spot has become a cornfield now, and in that capacity serves as his monument. 'Let us go to Europe,' the restless young Americans exclaim, 'to the lands of our forefathers, the countries of sweet memories and romance. Expressed in one brief word—Europe.'

"Our aircraft is ready to take off. It is crowded, for most people go by air as it is faster than a sea voyage. The submarine cable has wired ahead the number of aerial passengers. Soon the coast of Ireland is in sight, but the passengers remain asleep—they have left orders not to be called until they are over England. That is where they will first step down on European soil—in Shakespeare land, as it is also called, or the country of politics and industry, as others see it. We spend one whole day here, which is as much time as busy people can allot to the great countries England and Scotland.

"We continue our trip via the cross-Channel tunnel to France, the home of Charlemagne and Napoleon. Some bring up the name of Molière and others refer to the classic and romantic days of bygone times. We pay our respects to warriors, poets, and scientists who are barely recalled any longer but once lived and achieved in the cradle of Europe that is Paris.

"Our aircraft proceeds to the country whence Columbus set out for America, where Cortez was born and Calderón created his dramatic and flowery poetry. Charming, dark-eyed women work and play in the thriving valleys, and old songs tell the story of the Cid and Alhambra.

The drawings of the Danish artist Vilhelm Pedersen are considered by many to be among the best and most inspired of those made to illustrate Andersen's fairy tales. Here is a drawing he made for Andersen's essay on travel in the future.

"Our aircraft next takes us to Italy and the spot where stood ancient and eternal Rome. Much has vanished now. The Campagna is but a desert, and of Saint Peter's Church there remains only a solitary wall in ruins. Its genuineness is even doubted.

"Next we go on to Greece to spend a night at the de luxe hotel atop Mount Olympus, so that later we can say we were there. Then on to the Bosporus for a few hours of rest and a visit to the site of Byzantium. Poor fishermen there now spread their nets where legend has it the Turks in former days retreated to their harems.

"The fast-flowing Danube is lined with the ruins of mighty cities, and we cross other towns that are no more. Occasionally we pass an historic site. Some places will not become important until later on and others have nothing to distinguish them, but still our aircraft alights and then takes off again, in order that we may see everything.

"Germany now stretches below us. It is a tightly woven network of railroads and canals. Here is where Luther delivered his sermons, Goethe wrote, and Mozart composed. A single day is devoted to Germany, and another to Scandinavia—that is, the lands of Oersted and Linnaeus and the country of the Vikings in days long gone by. It is still inhabited by a hardy race.

"We pass Iceland as we approach the end of our air journey. Many of its geysers are hot no longer, and Hekla now is extinct, but like the eternal sagas, this everlasting rocky island stands firmly planted in the ocean that pays it tribute by encircling it with foam.

"Young Americans are correct in saying, 'There's plenty to see in Europe.' They are likewise justified in adding, 'And we saw it all in one week.' To prove their point, they quote the travel guide entitled *Europe Seen in Eight Days.*"

Jumping by Parachute

The parachute antedates the balloon —barnstorming Venetian acrobats are reported to have made parachute jumps in the sixteenth century.

When ballooning became a popular pastime and accidents began to occur, it was a natural development that the parachute and the balloon would be teamed, for thereby aeronauts had a lifesaver to fall back on in an emergency. Jacques Garnerin was one of the pioneers. He made the first parachute jump from a balloon on October 22, 1797. Another skybird, Jean-Pierre Blanchard, soon followed suit. Before long, parachute jumps became an integral part of many balloon ascensions.

One way the parachute could be attached was beneath the gas-containing bag, whence it could be released in an emergency, or as a stunt, and would drop to the ground with the basket.

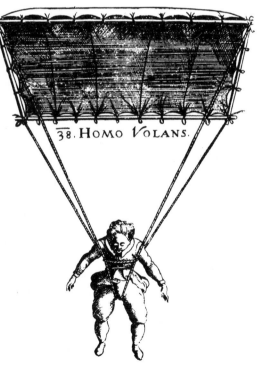

The first picture of a parachute—"Homo Volans" ("the flying man") from Fausto Veranzio's book Machinae Novae (New Machines), *1615.*

In 1837 an English inventor, Robert Cocking, conceived the disastrous idea of shaping a parachute like an inverted umbrella. He persuaded England's outstanding balloon pilot of the time, Charles Green, to ascend with him. Cocking jumped from a high altitude. According to a contemporary report, "Cocking was projected through the air like an arrow." When found, his body was shapelessly mangled. The picture shows his descent in the parachute that failed.

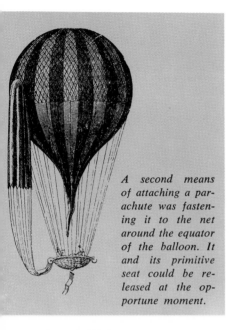

A second means of attaching a parachute was fastening it to the net around the equator of the balloon. It and its primitive seat could be released at the opportune moment.

ABOVE: *In the 1860s members of the Godard and Poitevin families were among those making regular balloon ascensions and parachute jumps.*

RIGHT: *Green's "long-distance" balloon, from which Cocking made his fatal parachute jump.*

Rising Above Earth's Miseries

Few balloon ascensions involved their participants in accidents. Most such trips were successful affairs, and ballooning as a sport gradually gained an increasing number of enthusiastic devotees in many countries.

Numerous books were written to describe the thrills and sublime experiences of ballooning. Camille Flammarion's *Travels in Air* was translated into several languages. He wrote: "Added to the joy of soaring in the air high above, and far removed from, all the miseries on land is a feeling of supreme quietness never experienced down on the ground. One notices no movement at all, but can talk and write as if sitting at one's desk at home. Nor do I experience any vertigo. . . . Butterflies swarmed around us. Hitherto I had believed that these tiny creatures spent all of their life down among the flowers without ever climbing to higher regions. Yet it is a fact that they rise higher than any of our birds. Nor were they afraid of our balloon, as the birds are. The explanation may be that the butterflies are so tiny, hence do not fear anything as colossal as our balloon. . . . The quietness reigns supreme up here. It is so deep and frightening that one is tempted to ask oneself whether he really is alive still. It feels as if one no longer belongs to life on this earth."

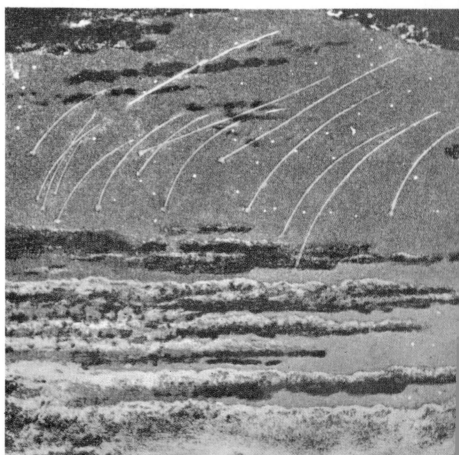

RIGHT: *This unusual scene involving so many shooting stars must have been an extraordinary sight—unless the artist was taking liberties with the facts.*

62

LEFT: *The beautiful mirror phenomenon has thrilled many balloonists. Camille Flammarion described it in his* Travels in Air: *"We were floating along, almost skimming the top layer of clouds, when suddenly the lower part of a balloon, almost life-size, appeared, along with its two passengers, who were easily recognizable. One could discern the minutest details, even the individual lines of the network, as well as all the instruments. I raised my right hand, and my twin raised his left. Godard [who was the pilot] unfurled our French flag . . . the phantom in the air also waved a flag . . ."*

ABOVE: *In time, balloons became quite safe, as well as capable of making long air voyages. In 1836, the English aeronaut Charles Green, with two passengers, Monck Mason and Robert Holland, M.P., made a record trip of eighteen hours' duration, from London to Nassau. Thereafter his handsome balloon was called "Nassau."*

Here Green reads an instrument at night by the light of his lamp.

In 1859 America's most experienced pilot, John Wise, accompanied by three passengers, set another world's record by covering the distance between St. Louis and Henderson in New York State in his balloon in a gale.

RIGHT: *Napoleon's monument in Paris, drawn as it appeared from a balloon.*

63

More Than Six Miles in the Air

Henry T. Coxwell, whose ballooning career lasted over thirty years (1821 to 1854), introduced illuminating gas for filling balloons. Though heavier than hydrogen, it was cheaper and easier to procure, and its use resulted in popularizing ballooning. Scientific ascensions also increased. In the early 1860s, several were made by the distinguished British physicist, James Glaisher of the Greenwich Observatory, who accompanied Coxwell on many occasions.

One of their ascensions (from Wolverhampton on September 5, 1862) nearly ended in disaster. They left the ground in misty weather at 1:03 P.M. Fourteen minutes later the balloon was at 7,200 feet. They were above the clouds and fog, enjoying bright sunshine, and continuing to rise fast—in fact, so fast that they were worried. By 1:28 they were above 15,700 feet, about the height of Mont Blanc. At 1:53 P.M. they had reached nearly 29,000 feet.

The carrier pigeons they had taken along could barely survive at that

One of Coxwell's balloons ascending at Leipzig in Germany.

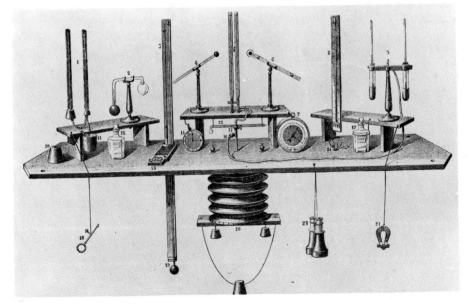

Glaisher had his scientific instruments mounted on a board in front of him. During an ascension on June 26, 1863, he recorded 756 readings and observations in an hour and 23 minutes.

64

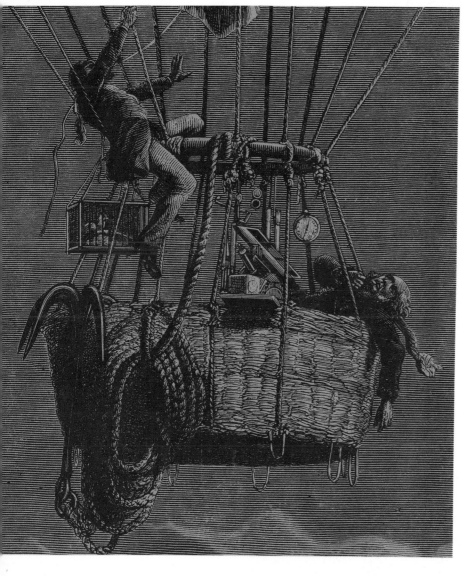

During the ascension, Glaisher and Coxwell tried to inhale oxygen through tubes fed from small container balloons, in order better to withstand the high altitudes.

height. First one pigeon, then a second, died from lack of oxygen. Three pigeons had been released earlier at 15,700 feet, 21,000 feet, and about 26,000 feet, respectively. In the rarefied air they had dropped like falling leaves. There was truth, after all, to what "Professor" Robertson had observed when releasing his birds at similar altitudes.

Coxwell and Glaisher felt no ill effects prior to reaching an altitude of 29,000 feet. When they had climbed

to about 33,000 feet, Glaisher became increasingly drowsy. His arms felt numb, too, and his eyesight began to fail—he was unable to read his instruments. Attempting to reach for a bottle of wine, he discovered he could not move at all. He tried to call Coxwell, who had climbed to the basket-holding ring to pull the valve, but found he could not utter a sound. An instant later he lost consciousness from lack of oxygen. Coxwell was about to pass out from the same cause—he did not

have enough strength left to pull the valve with his hands. Just in the nick of time he managed to wriggle the line loose from its ties and pull it with his teeth. The balloon began to descend and the two men were saved.

Coxwell also has to his credit the introduction of the guide rope in the balloon. This brakes the descent when the balloon lands and, when conditions permit, enables it to maintain a steady, low altitude in the air without the sacrifice of ballast.

The World's First Airline

During the Franco-Prussian War, in 1870, Paris was besieged. The Germans enclosed the French capital within an iron ring 50 miles in circumference, manned by an army of 150,000 equipped with 620 big guns.

Upward of a half-million Parisians were mobilized, but only a few of them were well-trained soldiers. It was not surprising that the French failed to lift the siege. Not only had the Germans established and fortified strong positions; they had reinforced their army. But though the Germans repulsed French sorties, they were unable to breach the surrounding walls, including sixteen advanced forts the French had built thirty years earlier. Nonetheless, it was imperative that new French armies be formed to come to the relief of the capital.

Paris faced a long siege and the privations inherent in such a situation. As always, one of the most pressing problems was establishing a method of communicating with the outside world. Under the circumstances, there was only one possible way men and mail could leave Paris—through the air by means of balloons that would pass above the heads of the enemy. Fortunately, some of the most experienced French balloon pilots—among them Nadar, Godard, the Tissandier brothers, de Fonvielle, Mangin, and Durouf—were gathered in Paris. With due speed, balloon mail service was organized under the management of Postmaster General Rampont, and simultaneously the manufacture of balloons was begun on a large scale.

Large railroad stations—the northern one is shown—were used for manufacturing balloons. Seamstresses and basket weavers worked around the clock. The spacious terminals were well suited for drying balloon covers after they had been varnished. And these buildings would otherwise have stood idle, since no trains were running.

Boulevard Montmartre during the siege of Paris. (Illustrated News, 1870.)

DIRECTION GÉNÉRALE DES POSTES.

AVIS AU PUBLIC.

Le Gouvernement de la défense nationale a rendu, sous la date du 26 septembre, les deux décrets dont la teneur suit :

PREMIER DÉCRET.

ART. 1ᵉʳ. L'Administration des Postes est autorisée à expédier par la voie d'aérostats montés les lettres ordinaires à destination de la France, de l'Algérie et de l'étranger.

ART. 2. Le poids des lettres expédiées par les aérostats ne devra pas dépasser 4 grammes.

La taxe à percevoir pour le transport de ces lettres reste fixée à 20 centimes.

L'affranchissement en est obligatoire.

ART. 3. Le Ministre des finances est chargé de l'exécution du présent décret.

(*Suivent les signatures.*)

DEUXIÈME DÉCRET.

ART. 1ᵉʳ. L'Administration des Postes est autorisée à transporter par la voie d'aérostats libres et non montés des cartes-postes portant sur l'une des faces l'adresse du destinataire et sur l'autre la correspondance du public.

ART. 2. Les cartes-postes sont en carton vélin du poids de 3 grammes au maximum et de 11 centimètres de long sur 7 centimètres de large.

ART. 3. L'affranchissement des cartes-postes est obligatoire.

La taxe à percevoir est de 10 centimes pour la France et l'Algérie.

Le tarif des lettres ordinaires est applicable aux cartes-postes à destination de l'étranger.

ART. 4. Le Gouvernement se réserve la faculté de retenir toute carte-poste qui contiendrait des renseignements de nature à être utilisés par l'ennemi

Postmaster General's poster announcing the terms and conditions of sending mail by balloon.

67

Mail Service by Balloon

On September 23, 1870—four days after Paris was completely besieged—a balloon piloted by Jules Durouf ascended with its car filled with mail. Three hours later, it landed outside the occupied territory, in Evreux. Durouf carried pigeons too, which returned to announce his successful landing and report conditions elsewhere in France. More balloons followed the lead of the first one in rapid succession. During the four months of the siege, a total of 163 people and almost 3,000,000 letters weighing nine tons left Paris.

Several prominent persons availed themselves of this balloon service, among them the Minister of Interior Affairs, Léon Gambetta. He had been against the declaration of war on Germany, but now he took an active part in the military activities. Gambetta determined to raise a new army wherewith to relieve Paris. He succeeded in reaching Tours, the new seat of the French government, and there gradually organized an army of 250,000 men, which advanced toward Paris, still holding out against the Germans.

According to Gambetta's plans, the attack by his army would be coordinated with one by the troops penned up in Paris, and would thus subject the Prussian forces to a crossfire. He awaited word from Paris about the readiness of the troops there, which was to be sent him by balloon courier. There is still discussion about whether this plan miscarried because the balloon message failed to arrive on time. It was entrusted to a new and hastily trained balloon pilot, Captain Rollier, and his assistant, Léon Bezier, whose story will be told in the following pages.

A mail balloon is readied for night departure. When the Germans fired at the balloons leaving Paris in the daytime, the ascensions were shifted to night. Two men in the foreground handle the cage of carrier pigeons, which brought back messages of microscopic size. These were projected on a screen (as film is in a present-day movie theater) and written down individually for delivery to the addressees.

The commander in chief in Paris attacked the Germans on the prearranged date, counting on support from the army Gambetta had created. But this help failed to arrive, and the Parisian troops were beaten back. It was evident that Gambetta had not received the message sent him via mail balloon.

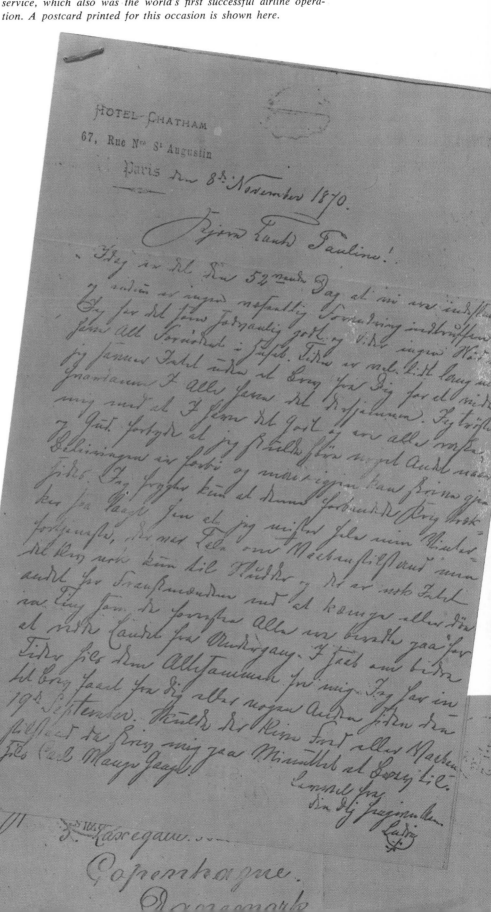

Rooftop observation posts were established in Paris, and watchers kept notes on the direction taken by departing balloons.

From Paris to Telemark by Air

What happened to Captain Rollier and his companion, Léon Bezier, who ascended in the "Ville d'Orléans" to carry a message to Gambetta that would coordinate the attack of his army with that of the besieged troops? Though the two aeronauts failed to get through with the message, their voyage turned out to be one of the most dramatic balloon trips made during the long siege of Paris. The "Ville d'Orléans" took off at night—what happened thereafter is told on the opposite page.

Captain Rollier, pilot of the "Ville d'Orléans."

The "Ville d'Orléans" balloon basket, now at the Norwegian Technical Museum in Oslo.

NORVÈGE
NORGE
TELEMARK

1200 Km.

La première traversée aéronautique
PARIS·NORVÈGE
24-25 novembre * 1870.

PARIS

72

At daybreak, after the long winter night, Rollier and Bezier discovered in horror that they were far out to sea. Their situation was desperate. They carried no food. The ships passing below ignored their distress signals. Only a German ship responded, and that by firing at them. Finally they encountered a French sloop that prepared to relieve them, and so they lowered their balloon in the belief that rescue was at hand. Unfortunately, strong winds blew them far away before the sloop could reach them. Hastily they dropped all their ballast and a bundle of newspapers, and climbed to 12,000 feet, where they were carried along at a rapid pace, at times rising still higher, then descending somewhat, but always shrouded in dense layers of clouds. Death seemed to be their certain fate; they even considered committing suicide.

Suddenly land appeared below them, and almost the next instant their balloon collided with a tall pine. Rollier leaped out, and the decrease in weight caused the balloon to start rising. His companion was forced to jump from a considerable height, but deep snow cushioned his fall. After a long walk in a desolate mountain tract, the two men came across a small cabin. Inside were fuel and a little food—otherwise the cabin was empty. However, when they lit a fire, the smoke from the chimney aroused the curiosity of the owner, who was working in the forest, and he rushed back to investigate. The men spoke no Norwegian, but when Rollier wrote the word "Paris" on a piece of paper, the man brought someone able to speak French. It was explained to the two balloonists that they had landed in the southern Telemark region of Norway. Later, their balloon was salvaged.

LEFT: *In 1937, for a travel exhibition in Paris, the Telemark regional tourist association appropriately published a pamphlet describing this dramatic trip during the siege of Paris. Reproduced here is the pamphlet cover.*

The two Frenchmen reached a log cabin in Telemark, where they found food and fuel and established contact with the outside world.

A Plan to Cross the Atlantic by Balloon

John Wise, one of America's leading balloon pilots, had already made 446 ascensions when, in 1783, he advanced a bold scheme for crossing the Atlantic Ocean to England in a balloon, accompanied by Washington H. Donaldson, another outstanding balloon pilot who had made daring ascensions for Barnum to advertise that showman's traveling circus. In spite of the great risks that Donaldson had run, he had so far come through all his aerial adventures unscathed.

Wise first submitted his plan to several wealthy men in Boston, but none of them was interested in investing money in such a "fool's scheme." The publisher of a newly established newspaper, *The Daily Graphic,* on the other hand, was excited at the idea and was ready to provide financial help. He figured that such an achievement would be a sensation on a par with dispatching Stanley to Africa to find Dr. Livingstone.

A balloon weighing more than eight thousand pounds was built, and detailed calculations were made in preparation for the hazardous trip. Four men were to be on board, and though a number of other people were invited to participate in the risky venture, nobody accepted.

Here is how the author James Parton acknowledged the invitation extended to him:

"To the Owners of the Daily Graphic:—I have just received your letter. Good gracious, how flattered I feel. Not because this invitation was addressed to me, but that you ascribe such courage to me. It excites me so and almost drives me crazy to realize that I have been selected to be the official recorder of this expedition and thereby possibly chance to achieve immortal glory in pursuit of my call in

that cause. However, I am just now immensely busy, hence forced to decline the great distinction. It was so kind of you to think of me. Perhaps another time. Respectfully yours, James Parton."

The project met with still other setbacks. A trial trip was cut short when the balloon headed in the wrong direction and in a mishap lost the lifeboat slung under the gondola. In the end, the trip across the Atlantic was abandoned.

The two-story gondola had a cellar for stores. Note also the large cage of birds. (Illustrated News, 1873.)

At right, the drawing envisions the transatlantic balloon serenely setting out in full glory. The auxiliary balloons were to serve as refills, as the main balloon lost gas in flight.

LEFT: *The auxiliary balloons evidently had a second purpose. The picture shows how a crew member might be aided in inspecting the main balloon for leaks* (Illustrated News, 1873.)

Copenhagen Becomes a Famous Balloon Center

The Copenhagen Tivoli Gardens became both a popular rendezvous point and a profitable place of employment for professional aeronauts from America and many European countries. Annual balloon ascensions remained a favorite amusement there for many years.

In 1872 the well-known French professional balloon pilot Captain Sivel was engaged. Accompanied by his daughter and his mother-in-law, who was the mother of the renowned balloon pilot Poitevin, he ascended in his balloon "Colosse," which was badly worn. Thus, it was happy news to the family afterward when his percentage fee from the Tivoli ascension amounted to close to $1,000, a sum having considerable purchasing power at that time. Now Sivel could afford new equipment. He immediately had another balloon made in the Danish capital, which, in his pleased mood, he appropriately named (in French) "City of Copenhagen," after its point of origin.

Sivel became very popular in Copenhagen and was reengaged for the season of 1874, when he treated the crowds to the sight of a "flotilla of balloons" by ascending with his main balloon flanked by four smaller satellite balloons.

In 1873 Poitevin himself was engaged, but he made only four of seven scheduled ascensions because, while in Denmark, this otherwise most daring balloonist played it safe. Ballooning can be extrahazardous in the seagirt country.

In 1878 Tivoli engaged a member of still another famous ballooning family, the Godards. This time it was Miss Fanny Godard, who really was a married woman. She performed wearing an attractive sailor suit, a practical outfit for one in her profession, but it caused quite a stir in a period when all women always wore long skirts.

ABOVE: *An illustration in the Danish humor magazine* Punch *was made more timely by including Miss Godard's balloon in the scene.*

BELOW: *"Chicken feed." Miss Godard presented Tivoli a bill for $3 for "varnish used on a small balloon." It was duly approved for payment by two officials of the establishment.*

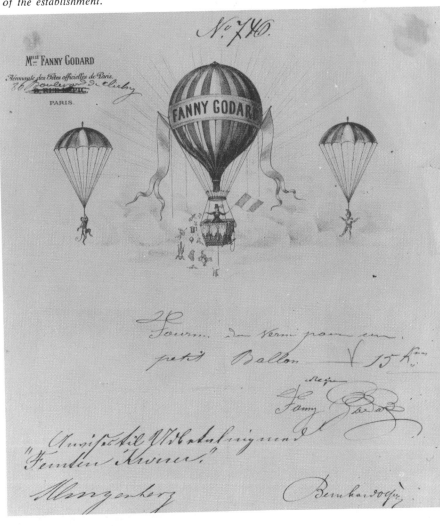

An Illustrated News *artist imagined this scene inside the "City of Copenhagen," 1872. The waiter at left has filled the glasses. The center figure, Captain Sivel, salutes two friends, thanking them for inspecting the balloon. The men in the background obviously wonder how they ever managed to enter through the small opening. We hope the artist misrepresented one detail: no doubt these people wore felt slippers or had removed their shoes—otherwise, their heels would have caused considerable damage and made this inspection for leaks in vain.*

The accompanying text explained that the balloon was inflated by an ordinary blower—that one used on farms to free seed and grain of foreign matter could also have done the job. Doubtless it was a strange sensation to stand inside the balloon; the surrounding trees and passers-by made a shadow play on the canvas walls.

A Tivoli poster announcing a postponed balloon ascension by Mrs. Poitevin and Mr. Sivel in the balloon "City of Copenhagen."

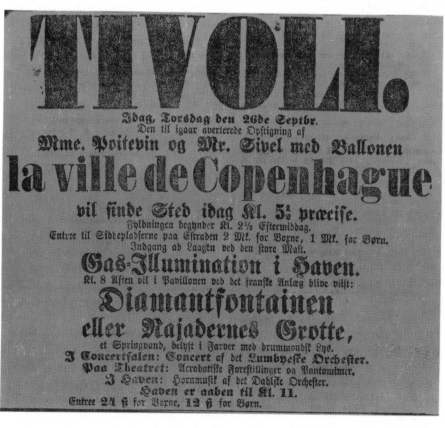

Two Lives Are Lost

The French Academy of Science gave financial support to a number of balloon ascensions undertaken to make scientific studies. One of these involved the balloon "Zenith," which ascended on April 15, 1875, manned by the veteran pilot Gaston Tissandier and the professional aeronaut, Captain Sivel, the third crew member being the engineering author Crocé-Spinelli.

This ascension is remembered in the annals of ballooning because of the tragic fate that befell two of the participants. We give the story as it appeared in *Illustrated News:*

They ascended at 11:35 A.M. from the Paris suburb La Vilette. The weather was fine, and a big crowd enjoyed the magnificent sight of the light-colored balloon sparkling in the sun like a crystal ball. The balloon rose rapidly. At 1:00 P.M. they had already reached an altitude of more than 16,000 feet. The temperature of the air was minus 5 degrees Centigrade. Occasionally they inhaled oxygen from containers they had taken along. Twenty minutes later, their altitude was nearly 23,000 feet and the thermometer stood at minus 10 degrees Centigrade. But the climb continued, and the rate of ascent increased still more after they emptied three of the bags of sand affixed to the outside of the car. All three men now felt pretty miserable. Tissandier wanted to reach for the oxygen container, but was unable to raise his arm. He glanced at the barometer and tried to announce that they were at 26,000 feet. However, he could not speak a single word. His eyes closed, and he lost consciousness. The time was about 1:30 P.M.

Tissandier recovered more than thirty minutes later. By then the balloon was descending rapidly. As he emptied a bag of ballast, he noticed that both his companions had fainted. He observed the temperature at that time to be minus 8 degrees Centigrade, and entered this reading in his logbook before fainting a second time. Shortly afterward, he awoke when Crocé pinched his arm and asked him to drop some ballast, since the balloon was continuing its descent. He saw how Crocé himself dropped various equipment overboard, including the aspirator, a heavy instrument weighing eighty

pounds wherewith they had intended to carry out experiments. Then once more Tissandier became unconscious.

At 3:15 P.M. Tissandier opened his eyes again. He felt completely exhausted, but could still think clearly. The balloon was descending rapidly, the car turning fast. Pulling himself over to his companions, he tried to lift them, but observed in horror that Sivel's eyes were glazed and his mouth filled with bloody froth. Crocé also rested with closed eyes, and blood trickled from his mouth. Both were dead.

Now Tissandier became aware of the strong wind blowing. The balloon was at an altitude of 19,600 feet, and he dropped two bags of sand. Yet it continued to descend rapidly. He managed to release the anchor before they hit the ground with a great crash. It felt as if the bag must have been squashed like a pancake, but the anchor had not caught hold and the balloon rose again. The car was dragged roughly across the fields, the bodies of the two dead men being flung from one side to the other. Tissandier finally succeeded in pulling the valve line to discharge the gas, and the balloon came to rest in a tree.

The landing had been made near the village of Ciron in the Indre region, and the local people immediately came to his aid. It was four o'clock when Tissandier again set foot on firm ground. He promptly collapsed, believing he was about to die like his companions. However, gradually he recovered. The following day he was able to send a report to the president of the French Aeronautical Society.

BELOW: The sad outcome of the ascension in the "Zenith." Though Tissandier recovered, all efforts to revive his companions failed.

A contemporary print of an ascension by Miss Godard from Tivoli in 1878. If the artist is correct, she unrolled her trailing rope immediately after taking off. This is not the usual practice.

When a Sailor Suit Was an Appropriate Outfit

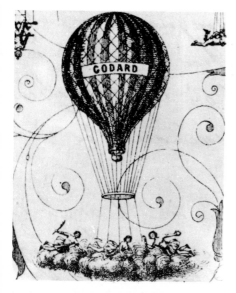

Miss Fanny Godard was such a courageous woman that only gale winds made her call off an ascension. When she did bow to the elements, the spectators did not show great disappointment; contemporary newspapers reported they "would console themselves by enjoying instead the good fare of the Tivoli restaurants."

On July 14, 1878, Miss Godard made her third ascension from Tivoli, accompanied by her manager, Mr. Martin. An unfavorable wind was blowing, and when the balloon headed for the Baltic Sea, they made a hurried descent. Luckily, their forced landing in the water was observed by a nearby fisherman, who came to their rescue. Of course the artist from the *Illustrated News* did not fail to depict the near-disaster (*below*). If his drawing is as factual as a photograph, it must be said that Miss Fanny does not look too happy, though she was gallantly supported by her manager and may not even have got her feet wet. Mr. Martin, on the other hand, is the image of a distinguished and imperturbable gentleman—still wearing his top hat, which must have been quite impractical for ballooning. Miss Godard appeared at Tivoli the following season, at which time she made six ascensions.

Miss Godard's rescue by a fisherman on July 14, 1878, as shown in Illustrated News.

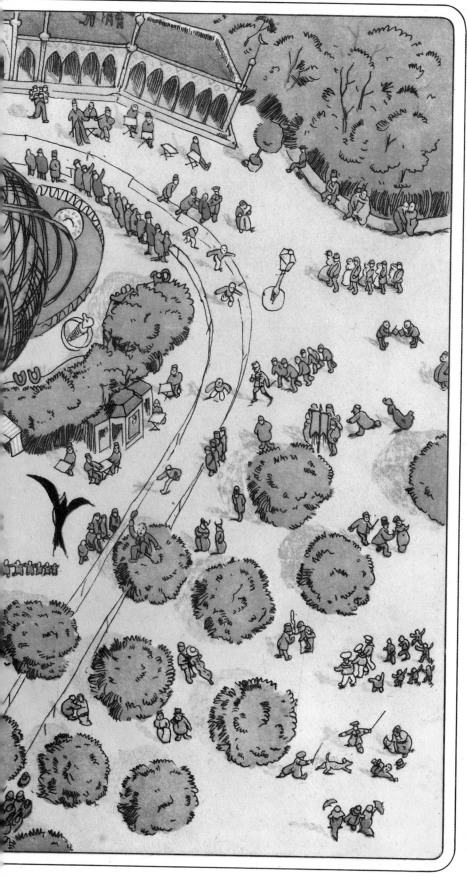

The Pawned Balloon

A balloon ascension became the annual midsummer night's event at Copenhagen's Tivoli. In 1882 it was the turn of the French aeronaut brothers, Paul and Eduard Damm, to appear there. (Paul Damm had also performed at Tivoli the year before.) The brothers made the number of ascensions they had contracted for, then stayed on, as they had become fond of the Danish capital. They had made good money, but they also knew how to spend it— so when they finally departed, it was without their balloon, which they had to leave as surety for their hotel bill.

The Damm balloon was bought by a Dane determined to become an aeronaut. He managed to make one ascension and was to have taken a passenger along, but by now the balloon was the worse for wear, and the freshman pilot barely managed to take off alone. It was just as well. The balloon quickly lost altitude, and the bold aeronaut was rescued from a watery grave by a vessel that came to his aid. That was the end of the Damms' balloon.

A balloon ascension at Copenhagen's Tivoli, as viewed from another balloon still higher up and visualized by the artist of Oldfux magazine. The translator of this volume has himself made balloon ascensions from Tivoli, and so can verify that the renowned amusement center may have changed in minor details, but the scene in this picture is little different from what one sees there today.

The Captive Balloon

A chained balloon—then generally referred to by its French designation "balloon captif"—was used for observation purposes, as already mentioned in connection with the wars of Napoleon. Similar military balloon activities took place later in the United States during the Civil War. When balloons of this kind have an elongated, cylindrical shape like a sausage, they are usually called kite balloons; they have become standard military equipment in most countries. For a number of years they proved popular civilian aerial lookout stations as well.

The Frenchman Henri Giffard had built the first steam-driven precursor of the airship of any promise in 1852 (see pages 118-119), and now he used his inventive skill to create a large captive balloon of 45,000 cubic feet capacity, capable of holding twenty passengers, as a feature of the Paris World's Fair of 1867. It was connected to the ground by a cable, which was let out and hauled in with a fifty-horsepower steam winch. One great advantage of the captive balloons is that it does not have to be emptied after each ascension. And by this date, more effi-

cient hydrogen-producing apparatus had been developed, so the cost of the gas was also less than it had been. Moreover, people by the thousands were anxious to display their bravery in public, and willing to pay for the privilege of going aloft to view the ground from above. Afterward, they were handed commemorative medals or suitably imprinted testimonial cards.

ABOVE: *In 1867, a humor magazine was inspired by Giffard's captive balloon activities to print this amusing drawing: The top-hatted gentleman tells the winch operator that his wife is one of the passengers. Grasping at the chance of undoing his marital ties, he asks: "How much will you charge to cut the cable?"*

LEFT: *Giffard's captive balloon was sheltered from the winds by high walls during the Paris World's Fair of 1867.*

RIGHT: *An* Illustrated News *representation of Giffard's immense captive balloon at the 1878 Paris World's Fair.*

Balloon Doings at Tivoli and Elsewhere

The adventuresome gentlemen pictured below in the "Montebello" chose to wear top hats for their ascension. Not only were they photographed beforehand; afterward they were handed a certificate like the one at the right, to prove their boldness to doubting friends and to serve as a memento of the occasion.

The men who tended the "Montebello" were an international trio. Alfred Godard was of the illustrious French balloon dynasty of that name; Laurits Johansen was Danish. The third man was the American balloon pilot, G. Loyal. He was in the Danish capital as manager for his wife, who was performing at Tivoli as a tightrope dancer at the time.

Until airplanes became more common, captive balloons were the means by which people had a chance to experience the sensation of being airborne. It was the French aeronautical engineer Henri Giffard who was responsible for popularizing flights in a captive balloon. Though the airship powered by a steam engine that he built in 1852 proved impractical because of the weight of the engine, his captive balloon innovations were a great success. His balloons were constructed of several layers of fabric, and that made them capable of remaining inflated for long periods. His balloon car was a circular platform that eventually was made large enough to hold fifty passengers. Such captive balloons were hauled down by a heavy rope attached to a steam winch, after they had ascended to a thousand feet or more.

The "Montebello" being filled from a mobile hydrogen generator (Tivoli, 1891).

Drawing of an old-style field hydrogen generator, supplied by Yon, the Paris balloon manufacturer. Through the pipes at (a), water and sulfuric acid were fed to the boilers (b), where they combined with iron shavings to form hydrogen, which was cleaned and cooled in kettle (c) and dried in kettle (d).

As already mentioned, Giffard's first captive balloon was a popular feature of the Paris Exposition of 1859, the Empress Eugénie being among those to go aloft in it. He operated larger captive balloons in London during 1868 and 1869, but the inclement weather in England and the occurrence of several accidents made the venture a failure commercially. It was a different story at the Paris World's Fair of 1878. Giffard operated an even bigger balloon, 108 feet in diameter, and in a period of six months some 35,000 people went aloft in it. Among his passengers were such celebrities as Victor Hugo, Gambetta, General MacMahon, Sarah Bernhardt, and the future German emperor, Wilhelm II, to whose eventual defeat air power was to be a contributing factor.

An 1891 photograph of the American balloon pilot Loyal, the Frenchman Alfred Godard, and the Dane Laurits Johansen.

Laurits Johansen and two of his "aerostatic" figures

A popular practice with balloonists is dropping cards from the balloon bearing the date, time, altitude, and location. The finder of such a card is asked to put it in the mail. This card dropped by Spelterini was addressed to the manager of Tivoli.

Poster advertising a Johansen ascension featuring four satellite balloons

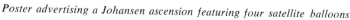

Laurits Johansen, professional balloon pilot at Tivoli

Other French balloon manufacturers were Edouard Surcouf, Lachambre, Louis Godard, Jr., and Gabriel Yon. The last two supplied many of the balloons that left Paris during the siege of 1870/71 with mail, carrier pigeons, and passengers.

Over the years, captive balloons have operated in many parts of the world, often sponsored by firms that produced French champagnes, to advertise their product. During the 1890s they operated in Chicago, Mexico City, and Buenos Aires, and the Paris World's Fair of 1900 featured no less than three such balloons.

In time, Laurits Johansen became the regular balloon pilot of the Tivoli establishment at Copenhagen. He made more than one hundred ascensions from there, in all.

Johansen had begun his ballooning apprenticeship as an assistant to Alfred Godard, who was in charge of the ascensions by the captive balloon "Montebello" at Copenhagen in 1891, but his career nearly ended before it began. When the "Montebello" began to leak, Johansen volunteered to climb the network to locate the faulty spot. Unaware of his presence on top of the balloon, Godard pulled the valve. Johansen inhaled enough of the gas so that he became ill. His skin turned yellow, and for a month his life hung in the balance. When he finally recovered, he was awarded an extra month's salary for his devotion to duty.

One picture on page 89 shows a poster advertising a Johansen balloon ascension with four satellite balloons. This event turned out a failure. In the windy weather the satellites began to tear loose and had to be abandoned.

Another illustration shows Johansen with some of his "aerostatic" figures. From 1785 on, for many years, the German Enslen brothers of Strasbourg launched similar inflated figures all over Europe. Many others followed suit. Such displays were often elaborate, realistic affairs that might, for instance, take some such form as a hunt in which a fox or stag was hotly pursued by a subsequently launched hound or hunter. Then fireworks would be set off and the animal would come plummeting to its death on the ground. The figures generally were made from goldbeater's skin and inflated with hydrogen. The procedure interested spectators just as much as the filling of a regular balloon.

Inflated figures on an even larger scale are still popular today, as evidenced by the giant specimens paraded in the streets of New York and elsewhere on Thanksgiving Day. Now, however, man plays safe by inflating them with helium instead of hydrogen.

Looking inside the "Montebello," which has been inflated with air so that the interior can be inspected.

90

ABOVE: *Even today the Ferris wheel at Tivoli Gardens features balloons above the rotating cars. Shown here is the earliest version of the Ferris wheel at Tivoli. The signs promise the passenger a commemorative medal after his ride.*

Fashions Reflected the Balloon Influence

The first balloon sleeves appeared on women's wear during the Biedermeier period of the early nineteenth century. After a long period of being out of favor, they reappeared strikingly in the costume of the fashionably dressed lady in the Gay Nineties, during the last heyday of ballooning. Fashion designers may not have realized it, but they undoubtedly were inspired by the general interest in balloon activities.

As usual, the weeklies made fun of the fad while it lasted.

Every Two Weeks magazine pictured a stylish Danish lady of 1896. Balloon sleeves were a fashion holdover from the year before, but the tinier waistline was new. The caption read: "The corset—this modern instrument of torture, as wicked and envious men term it—may well be misused."

This 1894 magazine illustration was titled "Modern World" in Denmark, but it was published elsewhere in Europe too. The magazine contained patterns for these balloon-sleeved dresses.

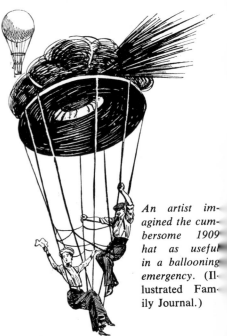

An artist imagined the cumbersome 1909 hat as useful in a ballooning emergency. (Illustrated Family Journal.)

92

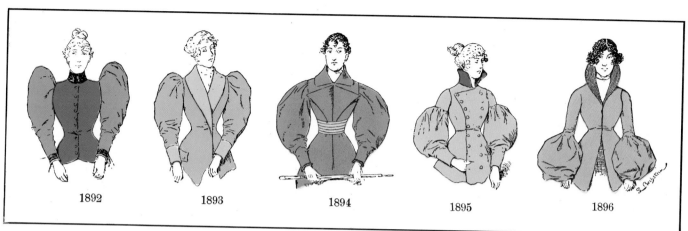

1892   1893   1894   1895   1896

In 1895 The North Star *showed how a modern elopement was staged:*

The sweet thing decides to elope.

A lady with balloon sleeves poses at a photographer's studio. At right is the outcome of the camera artist's efforts. (Fliegende Blätter, 1891.)

Her sleeves are inflated with hydrogen.

HYDROG

The restraining ropes are cut.

Away she soars, towing her beloved.

They are beyond the range of her father's wrath.

The balloon, long a favorite motif in advertisements, also played a part in the messages to be delivered. Above is an 1897 German advertisement. Below, at right, is a romantic French postcard. The young man has decorated the balloon in sentimental style, in preparation for proposing.

A balloon cartoon makes fun of the political power play. Financial, military, and clerical circles vainly strive to suppress the labor party. (Glühlichter, Vienna.)

Cornered, one grasps at any straw. A frenzied debtor begs the pilot: "Please take me with you. My tailor's after me!" (Fliegende Blätter, 1893.)

1900: The balloon finally solves all travel problems—short trips, weekend excursions, and long voyages. By 1900, balloons will replace both private vehicles and taxis.

NEWS ITEM

1892: The law against noise from piano practice was finally passed by a great majority. Hereafter, practice in the usual manner is permitted between 2:00 and 4:00 P.M. At other hours, the so-called "balloon for unskilled amateurs" is to be used, so that neighbors will not be disturbed.

1888: The Davidson family at the new balloon-restaurant.

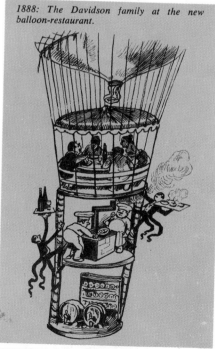

ADVERTISEMENT

1890: Accommodations are still available on "Pleasure Balloon No. 6248" for a lonesome gentleman anxious to meet a refined and sensitive lady. Replies to . . .

How the Illustrated Family Journal *looked into the future in 1885.*

95

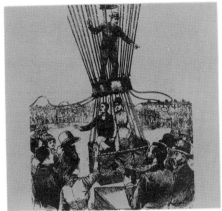

All during the nineteenth century the balloon was exploited as an attention-getter. In a number of cases—several in the United States—young couples launched their married life with an aerial wedding. Balloon weddings were sure to attract crowds.

The translator himself suggested to his bride-to-be that they begin their honeymoon with a balloon ascension, arguing that it would be both fitting and symbolic, since a balloon trip—like a marriage—does not have a predetermined ending point. He was turned down with, "No, on my honeymoon I want comfort."

France long enjoyed a monopoly on risqué magazines and the treatment of erotica. In this drawing from La Vie en Culotte Rouge, 1909, a dashing officer who has set the stage in a balloon car boldly challenges his topless companion, "If you're not afraid, I can still climb higher."

For many years an anchor was part of the equipment of every balloon. If a strong wind was blowing and the anchor took hold during landing, the car was likely to hit the ground violently. The anchor has long since been replaced by a drag rope. Two Austrian postcards from the turn of the century picture what might result when such an anchor was used.

An amusing picture from 1811 shows the kind of accident likely to befall innocents in the air age. At a later date, an automobile might have been shown instead of a balloon —and the same result depicted.

The Race to the North Pole

For a long time few geographic objectives were pursued more hotly by explorers than the North Pole. Strange myths had grown up about this region, but gradually people began to realize it must consist of one enormous ice desert. It would be of greater immediate advantage to find navigable waters— a Northwest Passage—in the Polar Sea, to link Europe, America, and Asia by water. Numerous expeditions set out to achieve that goal, and their members endured incredible sufferings in this grim and inhospitable part of the world. One of the greatest Arctic tragedies of all time befell the expedition of Sir John Franklin and his men when, from 1845 to 1850, they strove in vain to find such a passage. He and his 128 companions perished from hunger and cold. A decade was to pass, however, before their frightful fate was discovered.

All during the nineteenth century, Arctic expeditions followed one procedure. The expedition vessel would penetrate as far north in the Polar Sea as possible. Then, held in the clutch of the ice masses and unable to proceed, it ran the risk of being crushed. So it became a tempting idea to turn to the balloon for reaching the North Pole. There would be no problem in making aerial observations from above the immense stretches of impassable ice, but dared one risk drifting above them at the whim of the prevailing winds?

The Norwegian Fridtjof Nansen was one of many explorers hoping to reach the North Pole. But for the time being—toward the end of the 1880s—as a preliminary, he attempted to cross the inland ice of Greenland with five companions.

North Star magazine published the two pictures shown here. They were based on observations during a previous Danish expedition there, and made the explorer Peter Eberlin doubt that Nansen would be completely successful.

"Can their grandiose scheme be carried out?" Eberlin asked in the magazine, and proceeded to answer himself. "I greatly doubt that it can. To begin with, it is not likely Nansen will succeed in getting ashore on the inhospitable east coast of Greenland. And even if he manages to land there, I consider it most doubtful that he will be able to cross the inland ice." Eberlin referred to these pictures to back up his statements, since they showed the difficult conditions Nansen would face in the ice fields.

However, Eberlin and other skeptics were proved wrong.

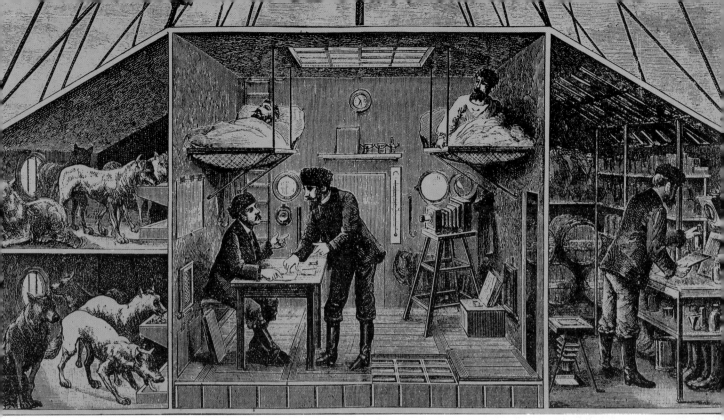

A French Plan

The first plan of any merit for reaching the North Pole by balloon was advanced in France in 1890. The balloon was to be named "Sivel" in memory of the aeronaut who perished in the "Zenith" (see pages 78/79). That same year, *Illustrated News* published this report of the plan:

Two young men barely in their thirties, the aeronaut Besançon and the astronomer Hermite, are to head the venture. We bring you the main particulars of their plan:

A mighty balloon nearly 20,000 cubic yards in size is to be built. Its carrying capacity will exceed 16 tons, and there will be a smaller balloon inside the large one. "Sivel" will be outfitted with several pilot balloons as well, which can be launched to ascertain the direction of the wind at different levels. Spare balloon containers are also to be provided, for replacing any loss of gas that may occur during the voyage. In this way, aided by anchors to be dragged along the ground, the sea, or ice surface, as the case may be, it should be possible to maintain a constant altitude during the whole trip.

The balloon is to be fitted with an airtight, stuffed basket suitably shaped to be pulled either through the water or across the ice. It can be heated inside by a small kerosene stove—that is, if they dare use the stove. The basket will hold a crew of five men—the two aeronauts and their three assistants—plus eight dogs, a sled, a small canoe, stores to last eighty days, water, alcoholic beverages, instruments, small arms, tools, and so on.

The expedition is to depart from a French port. Two ships loaded with the necessarily large quantities of equipment will leave next year and are scheduled to arrive at Spitsbergen by the middle of July. It is estimated that the air voyage may take eight to ten days, though it is quite likely that the balloon may descend in America or Asia within four days. The entire project may require six months, according to calculations.

The French plan called for a balloon dwelling divided into four sections. Two small rooms were to be kennels for the dogs that would pull the sled across the ice if the expedition became earthbound. If worst came to worst, the dogs could be used as food. Sleeping berths were to be fitted in the largest room, where scientific equipment, navigational instruments, and so on would be housed. There was also to be a combined darkroom and storeroom.

The roof of the balloon house was to serve as a platform for making navigational observations.

A Swede Joins the Race to the Pole

There was one individual who did not dismiss the French project for crossing the North Pole in a balloon as nothing but a brainstorm. This was the Swedish scientist, chief engineer, and manager of the Swedish Patent Office, Salomon August Andrée. It was his ambition to be the first to reach the geographical North Pole, and he was of the opinion that this could best be achieved with a balloon. Might the balloon not, indeed, be the only possible means of getting there?

In 1876 Andrée had visited the United States to take in the Centennial Exposition in Philadelphia, and on that occasion he met the renowned aeronaut, John Wise. Six years later, Andrée participated in an international physical and meteorological expedition in the Arctic regions. Meanwhile, he became keenly interested in ballooning.

With money granted him from certain public funds, in 1893 Andrée bought a balloon that he named "Svea." He used it for scientific ascensions, and in the course of nine trips lasting a total of 40 hours, he covered a distance of about 940 miles. With the experience gained during these ascensions, he grew even more convinced of the suitability of the balloon for Arctic explorations.

Andrée may have felt relieved when it became evident that the ambitious French scheme would never materialize. The cost of the French expedition had been estimated at 560,000 francs, a sum that proved difficult to raise. And now another dangerous competitor had appeared in the race to the North Pole. This was Fridtjof Nansen, who in his way had conceived an equally bold and unconventional plan.

In 1893, the same year that Andrée bought his balloon "Svea," Nansen set out on a voyage to the Pole in the *Fram*.

RIGHT: *Andrée (seated) plans the air voyage to the North Pole with Ekholm and Strindberg. Nothing was to be left to chance.*

BELOW: *Newspaper drawings by P. Hedman in 1895 depict incidents from one of Andrée's dramatic trips in the 'Svea.' A strong wind blew the balloon across the Baltic Sea. At right we see the way Andrée wound up in the belt of rocks and islands girding the Finnish coast.*

One of Andrée's ascensions from Stockholm in the "Svea." He always went up solo and generally stayed aloft longer than other pilots customarily did.

Andrée's most serious competitor in the race to the North Pole was Fridtjof Nansen, who was a skilled Arctic explorer. His well-equipped vessel, the Fram, *was reinforced so that he could risk drifting through the Arctic locked in the ice. Nansen set out on June 24, 1893. Nothing was heard of or from him for thirty-eight months.*

It was his idea to let the *Fram* become locked in the ice, and to drift with the ice from Siberia across the Pole to Greenland. If the *Fram* missed the Pole, he would leave the vessel with a small expedition and press forward over the ice.

Andrée, however, proceeded with his own plans, undeterred by Nansen's idea for reaching the Pole. On March 16, 1894, he met with the well-known Swedish explorer, Baron A. E. Nordenskiöld, who told him that he had long contemplated using a captive balloon for exploring the Antarctic region on his next expedition there. Upon hearing this, Andrée confided: "I may try to cross the North Pole in a balloon drifting with the wind!"

Baron Nordenskiöld encouraged Andrée, offering more than just moral support if the plan were carried out. So Andrée painstakingly made his arrangements. He calculated the total cost of the expedition would be about 128,000 Swedish crowns, a sum that proved relatively easy to raise. Alfred Nobel, the inventor of nitroglycerine, contributed 65,000 crowns himself.

The balloon was ordered from H. Lachambre in Paris, considered the most skilled manufacturer of balloons of that day. Other experts who participated in the preparations were the two Frenchmen involved in the "Sivel" project, and also the veteran balloon pilot and survivor of the "Zenith" disaster, Tissandier.

Andrée's balloon had a capacity of more than 6,000 cubic yards. It was smaller than the planned "Sivel," but Andrée proposed to have only two companions with him. The two scientists Nils Ekholm and Nils Strindberg were his first choices.

In 1896, Puk *amused its readers with a humorous presentation of the Andrée-Nansen race. Note the bellows used to blow air against the sail the artist put on Andrée's "Eagle." The sign at lower right warns: "The ice is unsafe."*

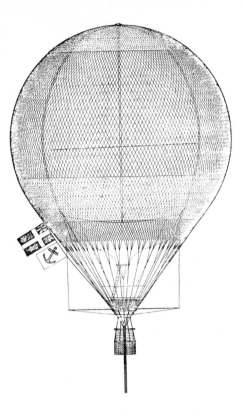

Illustrated Family Journal *made amusing suggestions about reaching the North Pole: Eskimos, already used to the ground conditions, might pull the balloon; or stilts could be used. Or rockets fired from guns might provide driving power. In reality, the Swedish government had leaflets distributed among the Eskimos from Alaska to Siberia to inform them about the strange vehicle, lest they flee from it instead of aiding the balloonists. (At the left are the drawing and text from the leaflet.)*

In the summer of 1896 a balloon (an object like that shown in the drawing) may be seen floating in the air. This balloon will carry a party of three Swedish scientists, who have been making explorations, toward the North Pole by these means. The Government of Sweden and Norway has requested that the explorers receive all possible assistance. Natives should therefore be told that the balloon is not a dangerous thing but merely a mode of conveyance in the air, just as a ship is in the water.

Natives should also be told to approach the people in it without fear and to give them all the help in their power.

If the balloon is merely sighted, the natives should be told to communicate the day and hour, the direction and time it was visible, and the direction of the wind.

If the people arrive, having lost the balloon, the natives should be told to give them all possible assistance.

It is requested that the travelers be supplied with passport and all necessary official documents, their names being:

Mr. Salomon August Andrée   aged 42
Dr. Nils Gustaf Ekholm   ”   48
Mr. Nils Strindberg   ”   24

When the North Pole trip was announced, North Star *magazine printed a cartoon prophesying that if bears provided the pulling power, they might turn on the balloonists and leave them stranded.*

To the Pole—to the Tune of "Long Live Old Sweden"

Andrée had intended to ascend with his balloon "Eagle" from Spitsbergen during the summer of 1896. However, he encountered a number of unforeseen difficulties, and finally was forced to deflate the balloon in the large shed that had been erected for filling it. "I felt haunted," wrote one of the men whose task it was to help prepare the departure, "but Andrée to all appearances remained undisturbed, although he was the hardest hit."

A new attempt was made the following summer, and this time they succeeded in taking off—on July 11, 1897. The scientist Nils Ekholm, one of the original members of the crew, had meanwhile developed misgivings about the project. He was replaced by Knut Fränkel, a thirty-seven-year-old engineer. Nils Strindberg, the twenty-five-year-old physicist, remained the third crew member. Shortly before leaving Stockholm, he became engaged to the beautiful Anna Charlier.

Strindberg described the departure in his diary: "One felt genial and touched, but not sentimental at all. Then Andrée called, 'Strindberg and Fränkel, are you ready to climb aboard?' 'Yes,' we answered, and mounted the balloon basket. Now my thoughts for a moment turned to you [he wrote, thinking of Anna Charlier] and my other dear ones left behind. I wonder how our trip will turn out. Thoughts come crowding, but I must suppress them . . . Was that a tear streaking down my cheek? But I must make sure my camera is ready and be prepared to throw out ballast and do whatever else is called for. Now all three of us have climbed on the car roof. This is a moment of solemn silence. Then the deciding moment arrives. 'Cut the lines,' Andrée orders.

Three knives cut the three ropes tied to the load-carrying ring, whereupon the balloon ascends and there are cheers from the ground. We reply with a 'Long Live Old Sweden' as we are carried aloft far above the balloon shed. It is a strange feeling—wonderful and indescribable."

By now Andrée knew Fridtjof Nansen's plan had miscarried. Though *Fram* had been encircled by the floating ice as Nansen had foreseen, the vessel had not been carried across the North Pole. So Nansen had decided to advance across the ice with one companion, and they had penetrated farther north than any others had, though they did not reach the Pole.

Now Andrée and his two companions hoped to reach that goal, which so many had suffered so much to reach, through the air.

The balloon shed is dismantled to enable "Eagle" to ascend for its trip to the North Pole. This picture was taken by Strindberg and mailed in the last letter he wrote from Spitsbergen to his fiancée, Anna Charlier.

The "Eagle" being checked for gas leaks before leaving Spitsbergen.

Knut Fränkel, who replaced Nils Ekholm
on the fatal trip, tests at Spitsbergen the
sleigh to be carried by "Eagle."

The picture of Anna Charlier from her
engagement card, which she and Strindberg mailed to friends before his departure for Spitsbergen.

The lines finally have been cut—"Eagle"
departs from Spitsbergen and floats toward the North Pole.

"It Is Not Likely That We Can Stand It Much Longer . . ."

Shortly after "Eagle" ascended, it entered a layer of clouds, and it soon became evident that the intensely cold air was making it difficult to maintain the lift they had counted on. In addition, ice formed on the balloon. Andrée made an entry headed: "Proposed changes for the next polar expedition." It read: "A means must be provided for heating the gas in the balloon, to prevent the formation of ice."

On this first day aloft, the balloon traveled at such a low altitude that more ballast had to be thrown out than expected. Conditions became even worse the next day—July 12, 1897—when the balloon continued to lose altitude and the car repeatedly hit the ice. Andrée had to sacrifice most of the floating buoys that he had planned to drop as visual evidence of having crossed the Pole. It was a tough decision to make, since it seemed to confirm the fact that the expedition would have a much more difficult time than anticipated.

On the evening of July 12, the car was allowed to settle on the ice, and at 10:53 P.M. Andrée made an entry in his diary: "Although we could have sacrificed more ballast, and the wind possibly would have carried us toward Greenland, we decided to be satisfied with resting here. We have had to drop

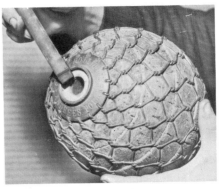

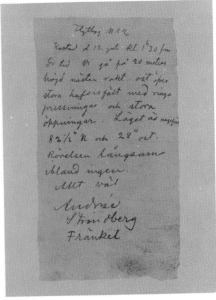

One of two floating buoys dropped from "Eagle," together with its message, which reported the situation on July 12, when the balloon was drifting eastward at a height of about sixty-five feet.

LEFT: *The Polar Sea, from "Eagle."*

much ballast and have been unable to sleep or rest because of the continuous bumps. It is not likely that we can stand this much longer. All of us need a rest, and I have let Strindberg and Fränkel turn in and plan to let them sleep until 6 or 7 o'clock if I manage to keep watch that long. Then I shall try to rest myself. I am afraid that I have tired them out and that this may cause their collapse.

"It is very strange to soar across the Polar Sea. We are the first to travel here in a balloon. When will our effort be repeated? Will they consider us crazy, or follow our lead? There is no denying that all three of us are dominated by a feeling of pride. We feel that it will not be difficult to face death after what we have accomplished. I wonder whether this feeling is not explained by an extremely strong sense of individuality, which makes it unbearable for us to live and die with the rest, forgotten by future generations? Is this what they call ambition?

"The clatter of the drag ropes in the snow and the flutter of the sails are the only noises to be heard besides the friction of the woven basket."

Next morning the voyage was continued—still at a very low altitude in spite of almost everything having been sacrificed that could be spared as ballast. Yet at regular intervals the car still hit the ice. When July 14 dawned, the balloon could stay in the air no longer—its lifting capacity was spent. The men were exhausted after sixty-five hours in the balloon car and had to camp for the time being. They realized they must now proceed across the drifting ice on foot.

Four carrier pigeons were dispatched on July 13, but only one came through. It was found by a quirk of fate when, two days later, the skipper of a Norwegian whaling boat shot a "strange bird" that took refuge in the gaff of the vessel to rest after being chased by two sea gulls. The bird dropped into the sea. Later that day, the skipper realized it might have been one of Andrée's pigeons, and he managed to retrieve it. The pigeon bore a message for The Evening Paper *of Stockholm giving "Eagle's" position and an "All's well" greeting.*

When the balloon landed on the ice, a dream died.

Across the Ice

Andrée and his two companions had reckoned with the possibility that such a situation as now confronted them might develop. To this end, they had provided themselves with a sleigh for use during their walk across the ice.

They stayed in their camp beside the balloon until July 22. Strindberg now had assumed the job of cook, and in this capacity he shot a polar bear to supplement their supply of provisions. They were not downhearted. Andrée wrote in his diary about asking Strindberg, "Do you want to wash, Puck?" and receiving the reply, "No, why should I wash when I did it day before yesterday? The remaining dirt will stick to me anyhow."

Before the three of them left to walk toward Cape Flora in Franz Josef Land, they emptied a bottle of champagne. But their good spirits did not last long. They soon learned what walking on the Arctic ice was like. Nor was their task made easier by having to push the sleigh ahead of them. On it they had mounted the boat and what remained intact of their elaborate equipment.

On July 25, Strindberg wrote to Anna Charlier: "We eventually stopped for the night here at an open spot. We are surrounded by ice everywhere. The pictures taken by Nansen will have shown you what these ice formations look like. Pack ice, high walls, and channels in the ice alternate with floes and melting ice. It remains one perpetual picture. It feels strange indeed to realize that very likely we shall be unable to return in time for your next birthday. It is very possible that we must spend another winter here . . . Poor little Anna, you will be driven to despair if we have not returned by next fall. You can rest assured that this thought worries me too, not for my own sake, since it does not matter now if I have to face heavy going. All I pray is that I be allowed to return some day . . ."

Yes, they had begun to be doubtful, and for good reasons. The mass of ice constantly became more impassable. They felt tired and weak, and on August 4 they had to face it: they were unable to reach Franz Josef Land. Instead, they headed toward the Seven Islands.

On August 29, Andrée wrote in his diary: "Last night for the first time my thoughts turned to all the lovely things available at home. Strindberg and

The campsite on the ice. At left is the balloon basket, and in the rear behind the tent Andrée stands by the boat.

The three men (from left, Fränkel, Strindberg, and Andrée) push the boat across the packed ice. Snapshot was taken with an automatic release.

Fränkel and Strindberg with one of the polar bears they shot as a supplement to their food supply. Andrée wrote in his diary, "We are surrounded by walking butchershops."

Fränkel, on the other hand, have long talked about them."

The intense cold and their hardships told on them increasingly. Finally they had to abandon the struggle to reach the Seven Islands and simply camp on the ice and let themselves drift with it. On October 2, they had a close call—the ice split near their snow cabin. Gathering their belongings in a hurry, they walked toward White Island, which was now in sight.

The entries in the diary became fewer all the time. The last one—written by Strindberg on October 17—was brief and incomprehensible.

Strindberg was the first to die. He was buried by his two companions, who doubtless succumbed themselves not long afterward. Very likely the frigidity of the polar night claimed their lives.

Packing up before leaving on foot.

The Enigma Is Solved

The sealing vessel Bratvaag, which found the bodies of Andrée and Strindberg and the remainder of the expedition equipment on White Island.

The sealer who rowed ashore to fetch water and made the sensational discovery.

Months, years, decades were to pass before more was heard about the Andrée expedition. As time went by, it became evident the three men had perished—but why, how, when?

The enigma was solved thirty-three years later—in August 1930—when the Norwegian exploration vessel M/S *Bratvaag* anchored off White Island, which has the nickname "Island of Inaccessibility." However, that year it was more accessible than usual because the weather was extraordinarily mild by polar standards and a large part of its eternal ice and snow melted.

The *Bratvaag* also hunted for seals, and it was a sealer who rowed ashore to fetch water who made the sensational find. Later, Dr. Gunnar Horn, head of the expedition, went ashore with several others. Andrée's and Strindberg's bodies were immediately found, and a large quantity of equipment. It remained in almost as good condition as when last used. The pressure cooker, for instance, still functioned perfectly.

Andrée's notes were found, too, and Gunnar Horn wrote later: "We were astonished at how neatly and distinctly everything was written—just as if it had been jotted down in a comfortable room, though the fact was that the writing had been done while they walked to their death across the ice."

Andrée's diary as it was found on White Island. Everything was written neatly and distinctly.

LEFT: *The zoologist Sørensen holds Andrée's camera. A large proportion of the plates could be developed, and they told their own unique story of the tragedy.*

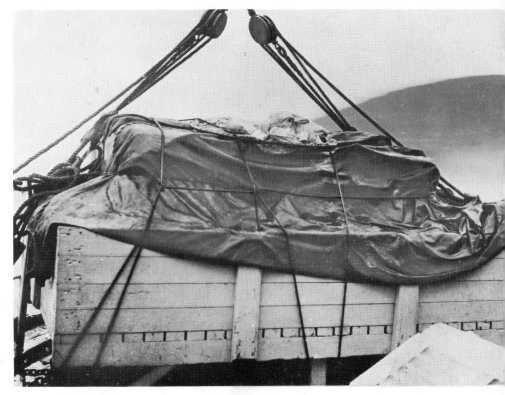

The Bratvaag *returned what remained of Andrée's and Strindberg's bodies in a simple wooden box mounted in the stern of the vessel.*

An Outstanding Scoop

Knut Stubbendorff, on board The Polar Bear, *with snowshoes from the Andrée expedition.*

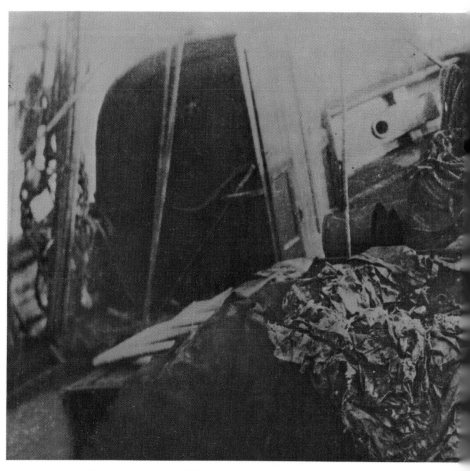

RIGHT: *Part of the findings, collected on the deck of* The Polar Bear.

More of the findings: the sleigh and the balloon anchor, as they remained on White Island.

A basket containing articles from the Andrée expedition. Among them are a towel and a letter written by Strindberg to his fiancée, Anna Charlier.

The fate of Andrée's expedition was news that created a sensation all over the world, especially in Sweden and other Scandinavian countries. The Norwegian warship *Michael Sars* left to meet the *Bratvaag.* The men on board the latter vessel had not yet realized what excitement their discovery caused.

Meanwhile, the Swedish reporter Knut Stubbendorff, with true journalistic enterprise, suspected that more might remain to be found on White Island. Hurriedly he interested—among others—the *Stockholm Daily News* and the *Copenhagen Politiken* in outfitting a ship, *The Polar Bear,* to go to the site.

Stubbendorff's hunch was rewarded beyond his wildest dreams. Not only did he find many items of equipment from the expedition—among them the sleigh and Strindberg's valuable notes— but also the body of Fränkel. Bits of leftover food were also found, proving that the men had not starved to death. Perhaps Sørensen, on board *The Polar Bear,* hit on the explanation of the tragedy: "I believe they met their death while asleep. They simply succumbed to the intense cold."

However, the mystery will never be completely solved. There is, for instance, no valid explanation for the empty sleeping bag in Andrée's tent.

Always Good Copy

An English book illustration shows a criminal escaping in a balloon. He threatens his pursuers with a pistol and manages simultaneously to express his contempt.

RIGHT: *A dangerous situation: the gas valve has stuck open, and the severe loss of gas makes the balloon drop at a hazardous rate. But this 1908 hero is equal to the situation—he climbs on the wooden ring, closes the valve, and delivers the passengers safely to the ground.*

In the years preceding the outbreak of World War I, ballooning was enjoying its last heyday. Ascensions were made all over the world—the balloon continued to draw crowds of spectators, having lost none of its aura of excitement and adventure. Magazine reports of balloon trips were welcomed by readers, and fiction writers followed in the footsteps of Jules Verne and created vivid tales of thrilling air voyages. But actual events often matched the fictional tales for thrills.

BELOW: *A real balloon accident, a 1902 fatality: Captain von Siegfeld of the Prussian Balloon Section ascended with Dr. Lincke, an assistant in the German Army topographical section, from Berlin in a military balloon. This officer was one of the most skilled balloon pilots of his time. A strong wind was blowing on that fateful day. On approaching the North Sea, the captain managed to land the balloon on the leeward side of a forest, but Dr. Lincke got one foot entangled in the drag rope and was dragged to death. This drawing appeared in the Copenhagen Illustrated News.*

For the Love of the Sport

Balloons were repeatedly suggested as a cheap solution to, and part of, a funicular. This proposed one from 1898 was to be built at Salzburg in Austria, but the project never got beyond the model stage.

When the present century dawned, ballooning had long been a popular sport. Annual rallies were common everywhere—to see who could stay in the air the longest, cover the greatest distance, or land closest to a preannounced mark.

During a balloon week in Berlin in 1908, no less than eighty balloons participated from Germany, England, France, Belgium, Spain, Switzerland, Italy, and the United States. Spectators estimated to number in the millions witnessed the magnificent sight of the scores of balloons ascending in rapid succession.

James Gordon Bennett, publisher of the *New York Herald,* offered a beautiful trophy to be competed for annually, the next year's competition to be held in the country of the previous year's winner. During the 1908 Bennett balloon race, the duration record was set by the crew of the Swiss balloon "Helvetia," which stayed aloft for almost two days and nights—for forty-

One of the balloons ascending during the dramatic 1908 Bennett balloon race in Berlin.

three hours, to be exact. They were towed ashore off the Norwegian coast, but the pilot claimed he would have been able to continue as far as Greenland.

Dramatic incidents occurred during that year's Bennett competition. Shortly after the American balloon "Conqueror" had ascended, it burst at an altitude of 3,200 feet and "plunged downward at a rapid pace." According to a contemporary newspaper, "The spectators became panic-stricken. The previous gay spirits of the crowd vanished instantly. Everybody visualized the bold balloonists as goners." A great cheer went up from the starting grounds when, shortly afterward, a telephone call reported that the pilot and

his aide were safe on the roof of a six-story apartment house in the Berlin suburb of Friedenau. The Americans, in their shirt sleeves, were calmly photographing their broken balloon when the ambulance stretcher-bearers came rushing up to assist them.

A similar fate befell another of the balloons, one piloted by the Spaniard Sotolongo. It developed a considerable tear at an altitude of about 6,500 feet, but he too walked away from the mishap unharmed. The simple explanation for these apparently miraculous escapes is that, when a balloon is torn and the gas escapes, the empty cover presses against the top of the balloon net and acts like a parachute, permitting a safe descent.

Man Is Determined to Set the Aerial Course

In navigating the air, the problem was that the wind, not the human will, shaped the course.

In 1866 the Aeronautical Society of Great Britain (now the Royal Aeronautical Society, the world's oldest) was formed. Two years later, it held the first aircraft show at the Crystal Palace in London. Keen minds in many countries were looking for practical solutions to the problem of dirigibility. By 1869, the Danish engineer Christian Nees had written in his *About Air Navigation:* "The air balloon has fallen short of our expectations. . . . Admittedly, many improvements have been made in the balloon, but still it can be used only for ascensions to entertain the public, or to make scientific studies where the primary need is to reach high altitudes. For those purposes it will always remain eminently suitable and superior . . . but as a means of horizontal travel between predetermined points, the balloon has so many faults and drawbacks that it seems impossible they will ever be corrected."

Nees showed great foresight, but his views were long considered too pessimistic. From the mid-nineteenth century far into the twentieth, it seemed only a question of time before lighter-than-air craft with an elongated shape would provide the best mode of travel.

LEFT: *The Frenchman Ernest Pétin work... on this airship in 1850. According to co... temporary reports, the authorities forba... him or anyone else to ascend in the "b... apparatus"—it was considered too dange... ous.*

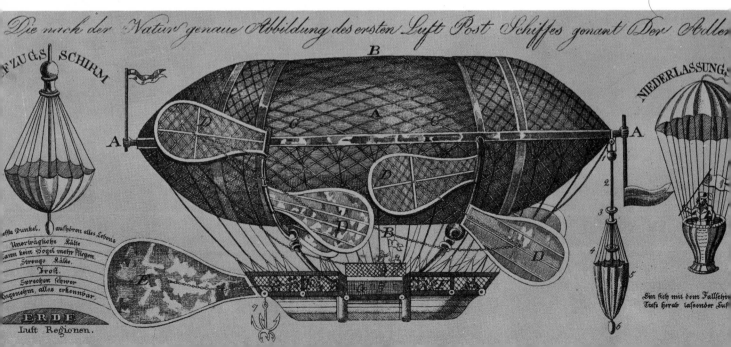

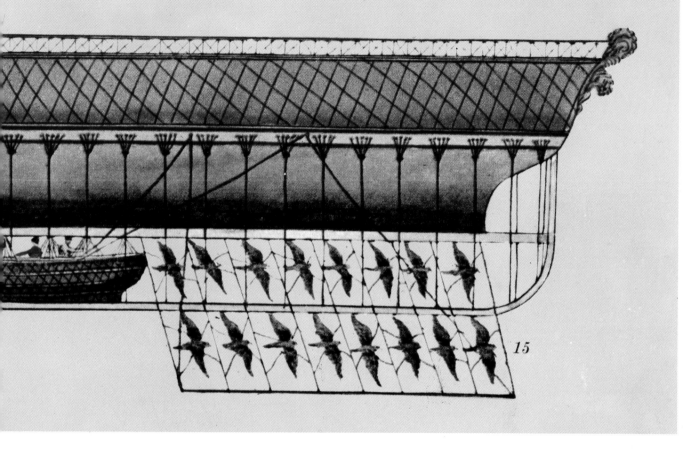

LEFT: *The French Colonel de Lennox was tenacious of spirit as a designer of dirigible balloons (or airships, as they came to be called). Cold-shouldered in France, he went to England, where he succeeded in finding financial support. This German illustration shows his plan for an airship built at a workshop in Victoria Road, Kensington, London, in 1835. Though it bore the proud name "The Eagle," it never left the ground. The labels identify the parts; the curved lines at left indicate the layers of air aloft where "everything is dark and life ceases to exist, the cold is intense and unbearable, scarcely a bird can fly any longer, it is difficult to talk, etc. . . ." Intended for carrying mail by air, the craft contained devices for dropping and raising mail en route.*

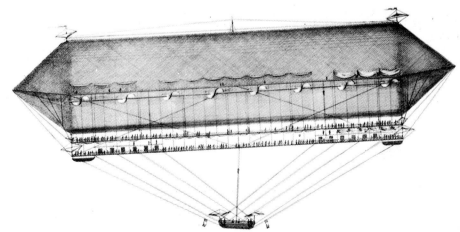

A rigid airship proposed by Prosper Meller in 1851 in Bordeaux. It anticipated later developments in several respects, but also evidenced several flaws. The lack of proper propulsion was one of them. Nothing ever came of Meller's proposal.

117

The Earliest Airships

Everybody was agreed that a dirigible airship must be "shaped like a cigar." Gradually it also became evident that some mechanical means was required for propulsion if the airship was not to be subjected to, and dependent upon, the wind.

When the steam engine appeared, it was only natural to think of using it for propelling an airship. But there was one serious drawback that proved an almost insurmountable obstacle: the weight of the steam engine and of the amount of fuel and water it needed made a load greater than even a very large airship could carry.

A skilled French engineer, Henri Giffard, almost succeeded in solving the problem. He built a small steam engine capable of developing three horsepower, yet weighing barely one hundred pounds. This engine drove a propeller through an extension shaft, and was mounted in a car slung a sufficient distance below the elongated and streamlined gas-filled body to make

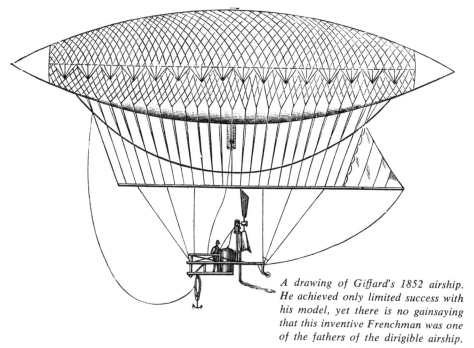

A drawing of Giffard's 1852 airship. He achieved only limited success with his model, yet there is no gainsaying that this inventive Frenchman was one of the fathers of the dirigible airship.

the Giffard airship a reasonably safe affair.

The airship made its first voyage on September 24, 1852. It quickly became clear that the small steam engine was insufficient to drive the ship against or away from wind of any force. Giffard built another airship in 1855, but it was destroyed by fire.

Small airship, shown above Hartford, Connecticut, in 1863, piloted by a man named Ritchie. Pedaled bicycle-style like several others, it could not be maneuvered in more than a gentle breeze.

119

Moving Against the Wind at Will

Technical progress speeds up in wartime—money is spent lavishly under the threat of danger, and the prevailing attitudes make risking human lives no deterrent. The Franco-Prussian War of 1870/71 was such a time. As the old adage has it, when obliged to, a nude woman quickly learns to spin her own clothes.

When the Parisians sought a means of communicating with the outside world during the siege, not only did they turn to balloons. Dirigible airships were also proposed, and Henri Dupuy de Lôme, one of the soundest inventors in the airship field, started to build one. However, he took such pains with each step as he went along that his craft was not completed until 1872. His plan called for a propeller operated by the hand power of eight men, which proved insufficient—a speed of less than nine feet per second was the maximum. Giffard's steam-engine airship had already traveled slightly faster.

The German airship designer Paul Hänlein was also inspired by the Franco-Prussian War. His craft had an internal combustion engine conveniently fueled by the illuminating gas in the gasbag, but that provided insufficient lift.

Finally the pioneer aeronaut, Gaston Tissandier, and his brother joined the race. They chose an electric motor fed by a large galvanic battery to drive the propeller. Completed in 1884, their model also failed—the battery was both too weak and too heavy. A contemporary report said: "Several obstacles remain. . . . For one, this airship can make barely any headway against the wind." As if that was not the main problem!

Hänlein's airship, which had insufficient lift because it used illuminating gas. However, it has the distinction of being the first airship ever fitted with an internal combustion engine.

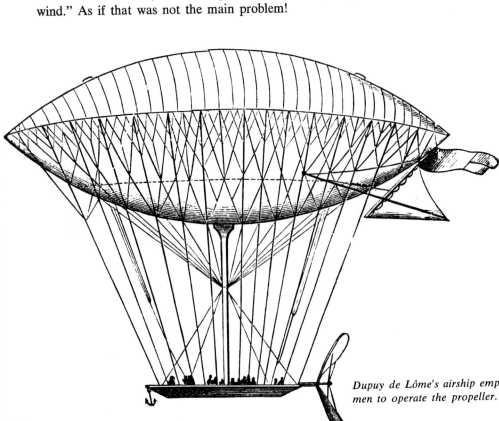

Dupuy de Lôme's airship employed eight men to operate the propeller.

The Tissandier airship was driven by an electric motor fed by a galvanic battery.

The Tissandier brothers in the control and engine car of their craft. The battery is between them. The shaft-driven propeller is operated through a reduction gear.

"Future hold-ups." (Das kleine Witzblatt, 1897.)

An Air Speed of Almost Twenty Feet
per Second

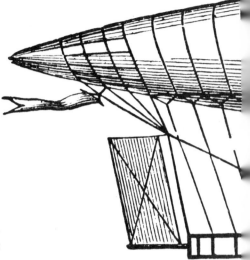

Again in 1884, when another dirigible began to sail the skies, it was hailed as a breakthrough. Designed by two French captains, Charles Renard and Arthur Krebs, it was named "La France." It too had an accumulator battery and an electric motor, one that developed 8.5 horsepower. The size of the motor, combined with the overall streamlined shape, made possible the remarkable speed of almost twenty feet per second. On five of seven ascensions, "La France" was able to return to its starting point, a performance not equaled previously. The press praised it enthusiastically as the solution to the problem of air travel, but the accolades were a bit premature. Undeniably "La France" was the best airship yet, but it could not make headway against a strong wind. A lightweight motor that would develop even more power was needed.

Then the first motor-driven cars appeared with their lighter gasoline engines. The Germans Dr. Karl Wölfert and his assistant Baumgarten were the first to install such an engine in an airship, but with disastrous results. On Wölfert's third ascension, the airship caught fire in the air and he plunged to his death.

BELOW: *"La France,"
the best airship so far,
in the air in 1884.*

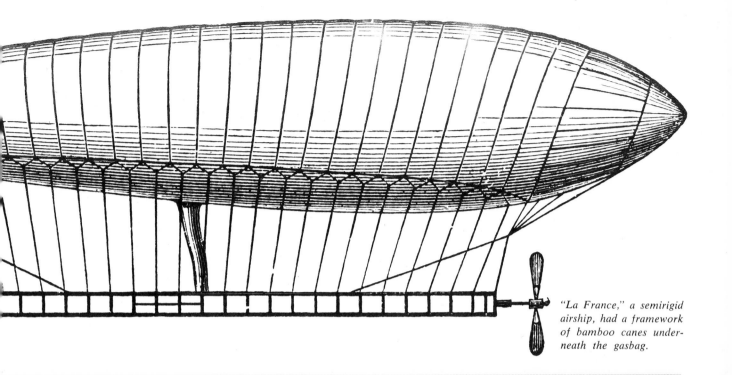

"La France," a semirigid airship, had a framework of bamboo canes underneath the gasbag.

The Greek legend seems finally to have turned into reality. Once again the human mind has won a new and important victory over the elements. The birds no longer rule supreme in the air. However, it is too early to determine the significance of this new invention and its influence on man's daily life. Certainly, though, it will play an incalculably important part in future wars. This is the reason the French government tries to safeguard its secret for the time being. It is quite possible that the new airship will completely revolutionize war. Henceforth, no fortifications will remain inviolate and no fortress will be able to withstand exploding bombs dropped from the air. Is it possible that armed air forces will now be added to all armies and navies, to wage war in years to come? Only time will tell.

The above is from one of the enthusiastic descriptions of "La France" (North Star, 1884). The Greek legend referred to is the tale of Daedalus and Icarus.

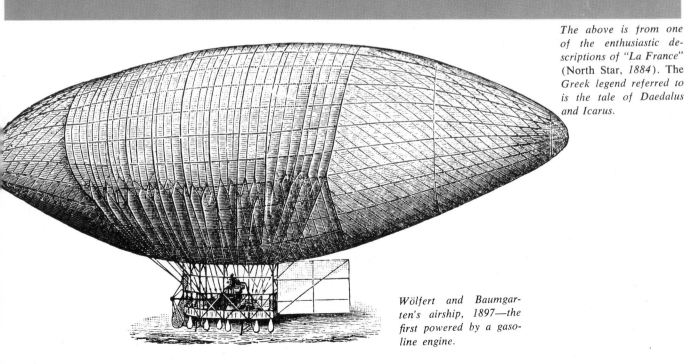

Wölfert and Baumgarten's airship, 1897—the first powered by a gasoline engine.

123

Encircling the Eiffel Tower

Alberto Santos-Dumont wrote a vivid chapter in the early history of the airship. Brazilian by birth, he was raised and educated in France and spent most of his life there. Aeronautics became his hobby after he made a balloon ascension. From 1898 on, he built a total of sixteen airships. Most were small in size and soon wrecked, but his spirit remained indomitable. He seemed to live a charmed life, always escaping unharmed from his air escapades. Once, the Paris fire department had to rescue him from a roof where his airship came to grief.

As soon as one of Santos-Dumont's airships was wrecked, he would build another, but his repeated efforts may not have constituted any real progress. His dash and enterprise, however, stimulated interest in air navigation. His most successful performance was on October 19, 1901, when he won a 100,000-franc prize for circling the Eiffel Tower and returning to his starting point, a trip lasting twenty-nine minutes and covering about seven miles—proving that his airship was truly dirigible. He distributed 75,000 francs of his prize among those who had helped him build the airship and gave the rest to the poor of Paris. Interestingly, the petrol magnate Deutsch de la Meurthe donated the prize. Perhaps he had a premonition about the vast amounts of fuel air travel would eventually consume.

ABOVE: *Santos-Dumont's airship in a ticklish landing in the Bois de Boulogne, September 1901.*

The control and engine car of Santos-Dumont's first airship, 1898.

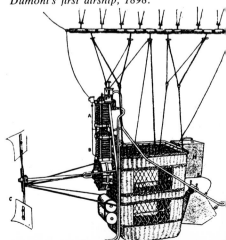

Santos-Dumont's airship rounds the Eiffel Tower and begins the return trip.

This drawing shows the commotion when Santos-Dumont landed his craft in front of his Paris mansion.

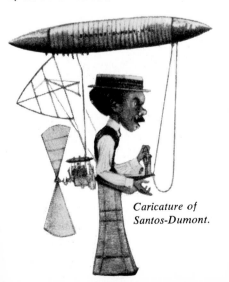

Caricature of Santos-Dumont.

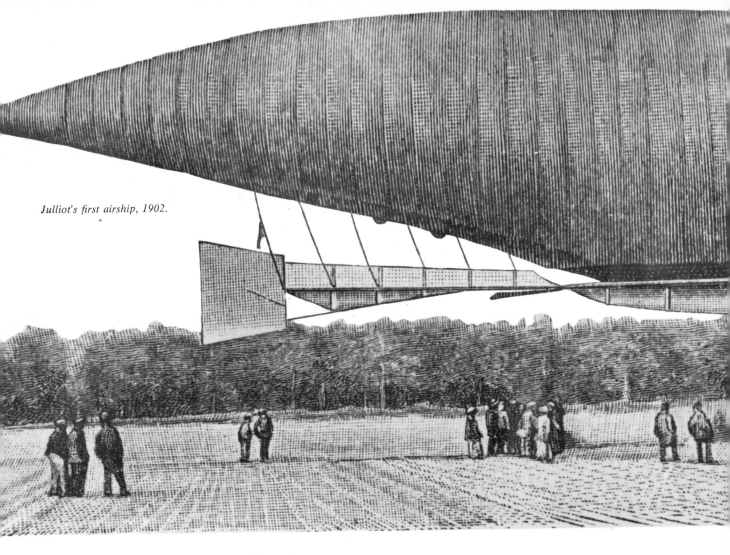

Julliot's first airship, 1902.

The Airship in Army Service

To Santos-Dumont, airships were a pastime. However, a French engineer, Henri Julliot, quietly produced a design that was to influence airship developments greatly, for he demonstrated impressively how well an airship can perform.

Julliot created a semirigid airship with a light metal frame supported by the gas-containing body by means of numerous ties. To this frame, the control and engine car was attached. The main innovation was a larger power source than was available before, a seventy-horsepower gasoline engine capable of driving the craft at around twenty-five miles an hour. This first model was called "Lebaudy" after the wealthy sugar producers Pierre and Paul Lebaudy, who were its financial sponsors. Its nickname, "The Yellow," came from color of the fabric used.

Between 1902 and 1904, "Lebaudy" made sixty-three trips and showed more reliability, stability, and maneuverability than other airships had. Deeply interested in its possibilities, the French high command not only bought "Lebaudy" but ordered a sister craft, "La Patrie," to be built with certain improvements. France wanted mastery of the air, to secure any military advantage that might give her. This desire may have been intensified by reports from across the border, where a retired German officer, Count von Zeppelin, was making rapid progress with airships.

Henri Julliot produced the first efficient airship of any practical value.

The remains of the French "La République" after its fatal crash, September 25, 1909.

127

Great Plans Miscarry

Balloon activities in America were generally on a par with those of Europe, but American airship achievements were inferior to those of France and Germany.

In 1906, an American newspaper reporter, Walter Wellman, bought a French-built airship with the intention of doing what Andrée had failed to accomplish: reach the geographical North Pole by air. Like Andrée, he started twice from Spitsbergen, but he was unsuccessful both times—in 1907 and 1909. He made no third attempt because the North Pole was "discovered" by his countryman, Robert E. Peary, on April 7, 1909.

In 1910, Wellman aimed instead at another great feat—he would cross the Atlantic in his airship "America." Once more he failed, coming down at sea prematurely. He and his crew were picked up in the lifeboat the "America" had fortunately carried. In the meantime, in 1909, the veteran balloonist and parachutist Thomas Scott Baldwin had built the first American airship of any merit.

A typical early, crude American airship. This nonrigid craft had a primitive framework slung underneath for the controls and mounting the propeller, which was driven by a small gasoline engine. The builder, a boy named Cromwell Dixon, was helped by his mother, shown here piloting "Dixons-Air-Ship."

RIGHT: *The hapless end of Wellman's first polar expedition in 1907. The airship, down at sea, had to be towed back to Spitsbergen.*

128

Thomas Scott Baldwin ascending in the first successful American airship, which he had built to order for the U.S. Army.

Walter Wellman, just prior to his 1910 attempt to cross the Atlantic by airship.

129

Ever Better

More and more designers and builders of airships continued to appear in Europe, and their dirigibles became steadily better. The French automobile company Clément-Bayard turned out a semirigid airship with eight sausagelike, hydrogen-filled blisters at the stern for stabilization. In Germany, Major August von Parseval made rugged, nonrigid airships and sold some to foreign governments. The airship industry had begun!

One name that soon attracted interest in airship circles was ultimately to

Count von Zeppelin

The first Zeppelin ascends from a float on Lake Constance, July 2, 1909.

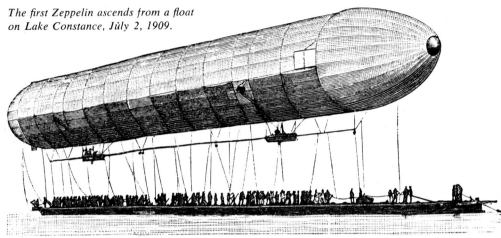

become predominant—that of Count Ferdinand von Zeppelin, who challenged France's lead in airships.

Count Zeppelin attained the rank of cavalry general in the German army; then (as mentioned earlier), passed over for promotion, he decided to retire. His trip to the United States as a young man, to observe military activities during the Civil War, had sparked his interest in aeronautics, particularly his ascension in a captive balloon in Minneapolis. Thereafter, the main goal of his life was to create a large, rugged airship.

For three years, with the civil engineer Kober as his collaborator, the count worked on what he considered a superior airship. When he submitted his plans to the German emperor and general staff, they gave him little encouragement. But, undismayed and unaided, he carried on. By 1900, his first airship was finished—a giant by previous standards: nearly 420 feet long and 39 feet in diameter.

The newly wed Count von Zeppelin with his bride. Isabella von Wolff (Stuttgart, 1869).

A 1908 German advertisement for wicker furniture predicted that even future airships would use it.

131

Germany Takes Over the Lead in Airships

Zeppelin airships were of the rigid type, with a framework of aluminum girders. Inside were a number of hydrogen-filled cells. If one or more of these cells was damaged, the entire ship was not necessarily lost.

The first Zeppelin was badly damaged in reentering its floating shed on Lake Constance. Though short of funds, the count immediately started to build another airship. He solicited contributions and received some support. The German army placed a few orders—too few to satisfy Count Zeppelin or to advance his cause as vigorously as he felt it deserved. But military authorities were skeptical and wanted conclusive evidence of a worthwhile performance by the airship.

Hoping to convince the doubters by making a trip of at least twenty-four hours, the count went aloft again. Within sight of his goal, engine trouble forced an emergency landing and, before repairs could be made, a wind wrecked the craft in a tree. The mishap proved to be good luck, for it aroused public sympathy for the count. This, combined with national pride and Germany's desire to outshine France, quickly produced ample financing.

The count and his airships met with other setbacks and accidents, though for several years no loss of life was suffered. The German army and navy both bought a number of Zeppelins, which had improved in performance as experience was gained in handling and operating them. Before long, a private German company ordered airships to use in taking civilian passengers on pleasure rides. By that time, to the public the word "Zeppelin" had become synonymous with "airship."

When World War I began, the average Zeppelin had a capacity of more than 900,000 cubic feet and a speed of about sixty-two miles per hour. Germany then had only a few military airships—the navy, in fact, had just one, the "L 3."

Count Zeppelin and his daughter, Countess Hella, in the control car in 1907.

An early German Zeppelin (the LZ V) had to have its nose shortened as a makeshift repair after an entanglement with a tree (1909).

The first passenger Zeppelin "Deutschland" was wrecked on its maiden passenger voyage. No passengers were injured, but the ship resembled a huge, mangled caterpillar.

133

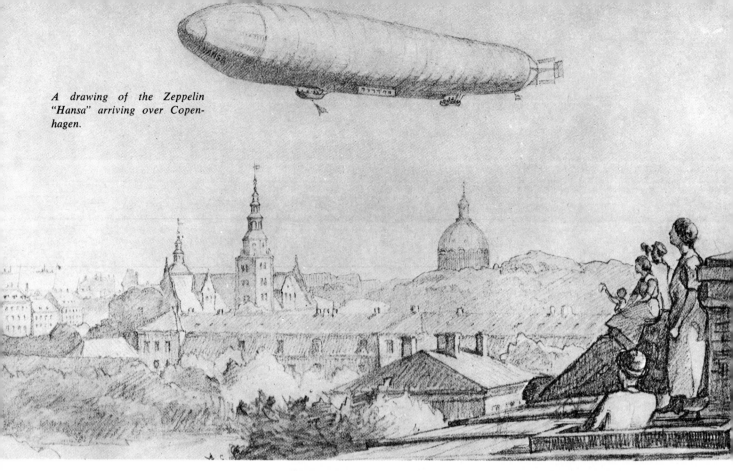

A drawing of the Zeppelin "Hansa" arriving over Copenhagen.

The Zeppelin Arouses Enthusiasm Abroad

Zeppelins were the first airships that could take large numbers of passengers on air excursions. In Germany an airship company generally known as DELAG, from the initials of its name (*Deutsche Luftschiffahrt Aktien Gesellschaft*), provided a civilian outlet for the Zeppelin yard at Friedrichshafen. A standard type of Zeppelin was constructed with open front and rear cars for the engines and control andl crew facilities. In between was a passenger cabin seating twenty, and a small kitchen. One early passenger Zeppelin, the "Schwaben," carried 4,545 people on 228 trips totaling some 17,000 miles before being destroyed by fire in 1910.

A sister ship, the "Hansa," made the first scheduled voyage abroad on September 19, 1912—from Hamburg to Copenhagen and back, changing passengers in the Danish capital. Dr. Hugo Eckener was in command; Count Zep-

Count Zeppelin bids Copenhagen good-bye as the airship takes off again.

pelin was in the control car but would not debark during the stopover. Copenhagen went as wild with excitement as German cities had. The Danish control officer on the return trip wrote longingly in a magazine report: "What a pity this airship does not have Copenhagen as its home port!"

The German postal service suggested carrying mail by Zeppelin in winter when Baltic Sea ferries had difficulties with the ice.

Copenhagen musicals of 1912 featured the "Hansa." This poster for a revue at Scala shows a leading lady singing while suspended in the air below a model of the Zeppelin.

RIGHT: A 1912 advertisement for light bulbs uses a Zeppelin.

Hvorfor?

anvender alle større Forbrugere

PHILIPS-LAMPEN

The first steps taken toward the creation of a German military airship fleet caused both envy and worry in England. In 1909 the British Admiralty decided to build a large airship, the "R 1" ("R" standing for "rigid"), modeled after the Zeppelins.

The airship shown here is being launched from its floating shed at the Vickers yard. It was known as the "Mayfly," and rather appropriately, for it was wrecked on its maiden voyage.

Prophecies and Wisecracks

There was no limit to their imagination when artists and authors used dirigibles as their subject. They looked far ahead and far afield in making fun of what aerial navigation held in store for us.

This book does not deal with aircraft of the heavier-than-air type, but it should be mentioned that the airplane, then in its infancy, seemed to hold little promise of becoming an efficient passenger carrier. On the other hand, the airship—that is, the foremost type, the Zeppelin—already had proved capable of transporting a sizable number of passengers to distant points.

Santos-Dumont's airship inspired the prediction that wealthy people would own private airships to call for them at their doorstep or, rather, balcony. (Home Journal, 1905.)

A Zeppelin decorated a 1909 party favor. The German advertisement suggested (even guaranteed) that the favors were the most modern ones imaginable.

How people with both feet planted on solid ground felt about it in 1909: the weighty lady says to her respectable husband, "Not even for a million would I entrust myself to one of those things." The artist of the Fliegende Blätter clearly picked a French dirigible to copy.

Flirting in an airship—a French drawing from 1909. The dashing officer in his fanciful craft has wisely doffed his saber, a hazard in such crowded quarters.

Movie producers, quick to recognize the attraction of balloons and airships, included them in their films whenever possible. Denmark Films produced a thriller, The Balloon Explosion *(1913), directed by Carl Theodor Dreyer, a skilled balloon pilot himself.*

In 1917 Northern Film Company came out with The Skycraft, *a very long film that concerned the imaginary air cruiser "Excelsior" on a trip to Mars, where it was given a cordial, peaceful welcome. The crew returned to Earth with a message of goodwill toward mankind—a contrast to the war atmosphere then enveloping much of the world. Needless to add, the airship was a trick shot. The scenes (see above) were taken against the background of Copenhagen roofs, from the model of the Eiffel Tower at the zoo.*

Balloons for Carrying Aerial Torpedoes

The German professional balloon pilot Rodeck ascended several times from the Tivoli in Copenhagen in 1885 and 1886, making quite an impression there with his magnificent navy-style costume, which he himself had designed. Later, he proposed using a flotilla of balloons to carry "aerial torpedoes" (as he termed them) in warfare—or bombs, as they later were to be known. He suggested sending five balloons, linked together, across enemy lines when the wind was favorable. Four would carry torpedoes and drop them at the right time, controlled by an officer and two assistants in the "pilot balloon." As each balloon dropped its bomb, it would be cut loose to float away. The scheme was never tried out.

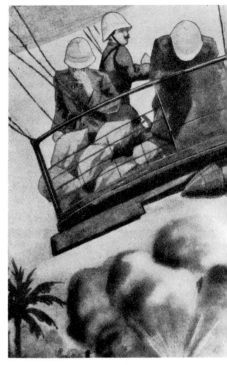

LEFT: *This is how Rodeck visualized his balloon bombing flotilla would operate. The approach altitude had to be carefully calculated lest enemy ground fire down the attackers.*

In 1893, the Japanese tried sending up a cameraman attached to a balloon. They soon learned he was overexposed.

138

An Airship Drops Bombs

The Danish sculptor Viggo Jarl sent dispatches to the *Copenhagen Illustrated News* during his stay in Tripoli in 1912. That was the year and place of the Italo-Turkish War, and according to Jarl, the first time an airship had dropped bombs. He wrote home:

"At ten o'clock in the morning we received reports of two Italian airships having been sighted. One headed unpleasantly straight for the little fort where I was staying. . . . There followed ten minutes of anxiety, and then we could hear the beat of the propellers. The full length of the large airship was visible as it bore straight down on us. . . . I fled to the oasis, but the airship pursued me and repeated every single move I made. Then the bombs began to drop and explode all around me and my terrified horse. That air monster stayed right above me for several minutes and let its bombs pour down. Some of them exploded with a frightening and sputtering thunder. Others were duds, and rested on the ground like heavy lead bottles."

When the bombing was over, Jarl found a wooden cylinder that had been part of a bomb. It bore a stern greeting from home, being imprinted: "*Defenseur Copenhague patente universelle.*"

ABOVE: *Italian war picture from 1912. It probably depicts the bombing trip described by Viggo Jarl.*

RIGHT: *In the Russo-Japanese War of 1904/05, the Japanese sent up kite balloons in an attempt to intercept Russian telegraph messages.*

BELOW: *The Danish sculptor Viggo Jarl in European dress, with his interpreter and guide and Turkish soldiers, in the desert in 1912.*

World War I

When World War I broke out in August 1914, France, England, and Germany all possessed small fleets of airships. The German Zeppelins were the largest, fastest, and most efficient, and the Germans planned to use them in aerial warfare. Yet the first bombing raid on England did not take place until the night of January 19, 1915.

In the beginning, airships were superior to airplanes in several respects, including the rate of climb. A number of airships were built in all the warring countries, but gradually airplanes were greatly improved and their performance became superior to that of airships. Consequently, airships ceased to be used as an offensive weapon, though the German rigid airships continued to render valuable scouting service to the German navy, and a large number of small, nonrigid airships were operated by the British as submarine hunters and for convoy duty.

On the opposite page are two drawings by the English artist Morrell. The left one shows how, at one stage of the war, a Zeppelin could approach England, obscured from view above the clouds. It would lower by cable, and later raise again, an observer in a car that projected just below the clouds, to make the necessary observations for bombing. In the picture at right, the artist depicts a German airship caught at night by a searchlight.

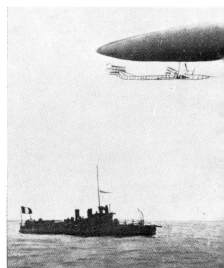

ABOVE: *A Clément-Bayard airship of the semirigid type scouting for a French destroyer in the English Channel prior to the outbreak of war. By 1914 France had improved her airships, but they were no match for Zeppelins.*

In two fields airships remained superior to airplanes throughout World War I: for scouting and submarine hunting. They had a wider range and could stay in the air longer. Thus, airships were able to give ample warning of enemy attacks. Here a Zeppelin is seen on scouting duty with the German North Sea fleet.

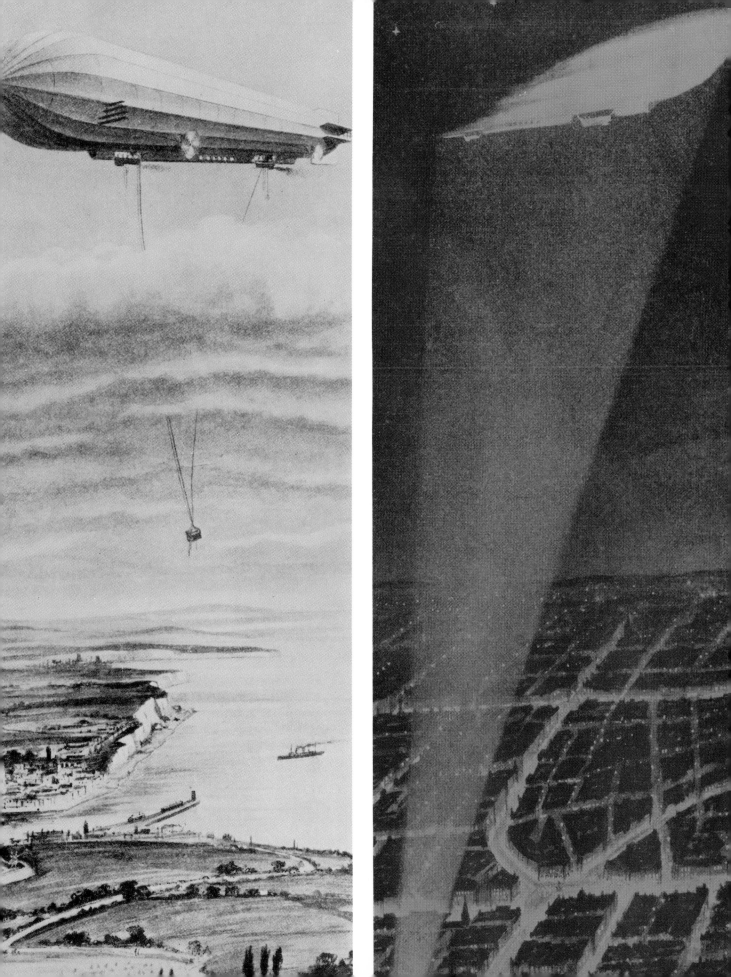

Water Froze in the Zeppelins

The first Zeppelin bombardment of England occurred on January 19, 1915, as mentioned on page 140. Two persons, a shoemaker and a housewife, were killed. The loss of these lives by bombing caused a greater stir than the loss of thousands on the Western Front. After this raid, many people felt England would now face a serious threat from the sky. However, the damage from Zeppelin bombing was not as great as feared.

Airships turned out to be quite vulnerable to attack by airplanes, which were improving all the time. It became necessary for airships to operate so high up that the water in the ballast tanks and the cooling water in the engines froze. They could not aim accurately when bombs had to be dropped from such altitudes.

English watercolor of a Zeppelin raid on London's South End, May 1915.

ABOVE: *A British artist visualized the "nerve center" of a raiding airship. The officer in charge of dropping bombs telephones his instructions.*

RIGHT: *A somewhat childish conception of the bomb hatchway at the moment of release. The bombs were slung on frames and moved to the release point.*

OPPOSITE PAGE: *One of the relatively few London apartments hit by an airship bomb in World War I. A policeman and the two women occupying the room view the damage to the furniture.*

As the war progressed, more German airships participated in raids on England. Sometimes these bombing squadrons might include as many as sixteen airships. England was attacked for the last time on October 19, 1917 —by fifteen Zeppelins, but half of them had to return prematurely when their engines failed at the high altitude of approach; the remainder suffered severe losses. Altogether, the Germans carried out fifty-one air attacks on England with Zeppelin and Schütte-Lanz airships, and dropped a total of just under fifty tons of bombs.

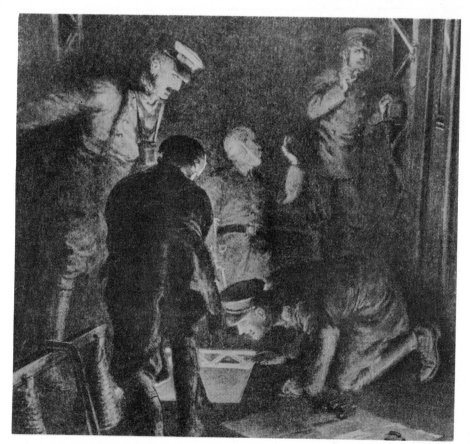

The Vulnerable Zeppelins

The greatest hazards raiding Zeppelins faced were improved English ground defenses, improved means of detection, and the growing skill of England's airplane pilots in finding the best approach and angles of attack for battling airships.

Lieutenant Leefe Robinson became a British air hero and was awarded the Victoria Cross in 1916 for being the first to down a raiding German airship on English soil. He commented afterward, "There really was nothing to it, for once the airship is detected, it's a goner. I only had to climb above it, open fire, and drop hand grenades."

The Germans tried to counteract such attacks by developing larger Zeppelins. By the end of the war, these had reached a length of nearly 230 yards and a speed of about 56 miles an hour. The new airships were armed with eight machine guns, two of them mounted on top of the hull, but their improved performance and armament were inadequate against attackers.

From four listening posts, the French took bearings to determine the position of an airship in the sky when it could not be sighted from the ground.

A Danish inventor claimed in 1916 to have invented a "death ray," or radio flashes, that could destroy airships. The English and French naturally were anxious for full particulars so that they could evaluate the Danish invention. Unfortunately for them, it proved to be a hoax.

Equipment was developed to fix the location of airship raiders. One means used by the French was sensitive listening devices for catching engine noise, which told them when to put antiaircraft guns into action.

At dawn on November 28, 1916, a Zeppelin was spotted over the coast of Norfolk. Four airplanes immediately started to attack the hydrogen-filled craft and succeeded in setting it on fire. Here is an English artist's conception of the view from an armed trawler, which also fired its antiaircraft gun against the sky raider.

A drawing of a crew member clinging to the last floating part of the gas-filled "L 19" when this German naval airship was forced down in the North Sea while returning from a raid on England.

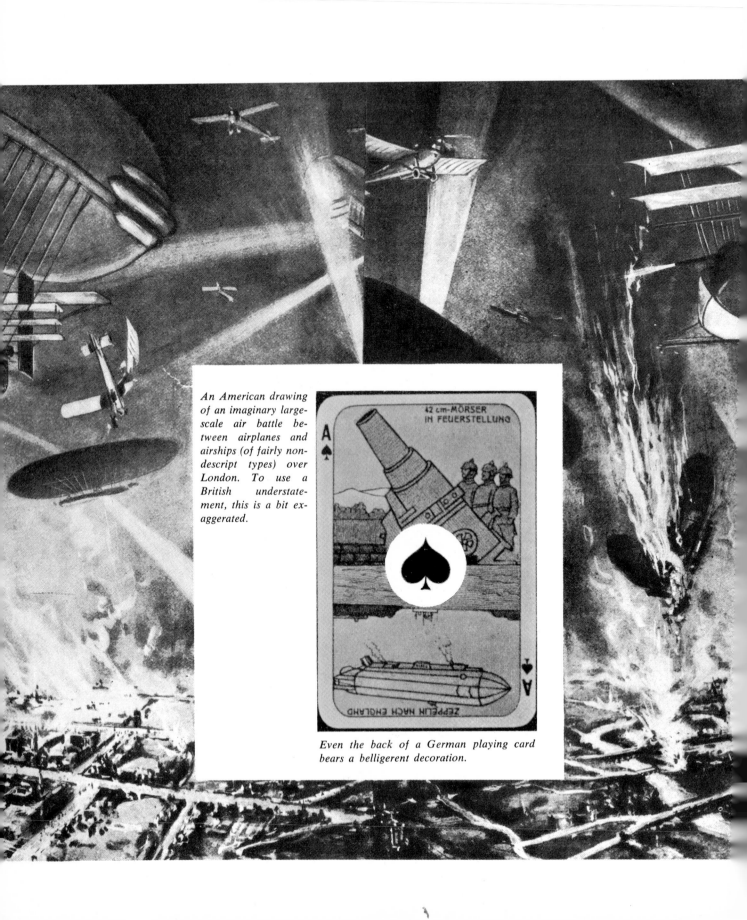

An American drawing of an imaginary large-scale air battle between airplanes and airships (of fairly nondescript types) over London. To use a British understatement, this is a bit exaggerated.

Even the back of a German playing card bears a belligerent decoration.

An artist's conception of a British biplane attacking a Zeppelin and setting it afire.

The Germans attempted to gain the upper hand in the air by turning out ever larger and better Zeppelins and fitting them with machine guns to ward off enemy aircraft attacks. Here a machine gun nest (as imagined by the artist) is mounted on top of the hull. However, airplanes proved more maneuverable and increasingly difficult to hold at bay.

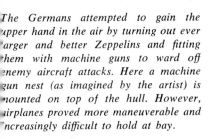

147

Kite Balloons

The captive balloon, unlike the free type that drifts with the wind, is held to the ground at an altitude determined by its tie ropes. It is used for scouting purposes, to observe artillery fire and troop movements. In windy weather a ball-shaped balloon is very unstable, and aerial observers in the basket often became violently airsick. To correct this, two German officers, von Parseval and Sigsfeld, developed an observation balloon that is named after them. Often it is also referred to as the "kite balloon" because it adopts an inclined position like a flown kite. The main balloon, of elongated shape, has attached to it a narrower, half-circular, auxiliary stabilizing balloon, which is open at the front end and thus becomes filled with air by the wind.

The kite balloon was used extensively in World War I on both sides. The Allies colloquially called this type of German observation balloon "The Sausage." Later in the war, it was replaced by an improved type designed by the French captain Caquot. One vertical and two horizontal fins, all gas filled, provided greater stability.

German antiaircraft gun firing at enemy aircraft. A Parseval-Sigsfeld kite balloon is at top left.

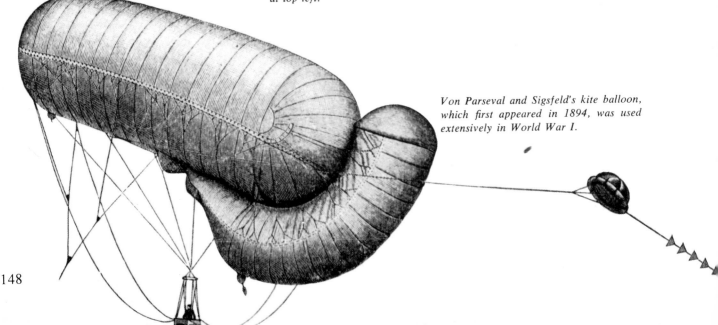

Von Parseval and Sigsfeld's kite balloon, which first appeared in 1894, was used extensively in World War I.

RIGHT: *A painting by the German artist Hans W. Schmidt depicting two French kite balloons brought down in flames.*

A girl wrote to her artist boyfriend at the Front for a picture of his aircraft. If he stuck to the truth in the sketch he sent her, it was made toward the end of the war, as the balloon was a Caquot. That should have reassured her—if she realized that observers in such balloons had parachutes and thus a good chance of saving themselves if the balloon was destroyed.

An observer jumps by parachute from his observation balloon.

Airplanes improved during World War I, but airships still remained useful. The carrier H.M.S. Furious carried planes on the foredeck and a small nonrigid airship (blimp) on the stern.

Now the blimp has been moored on the carrier. England had 103 nonrigid airships at the end of the war.

Experiments with airships as carriers were conducted in both England and America toward the end of World War I. An airplane was slung below an airship and taken aloft, as a means of combining the longer range of the airship with the greater maneuverability of the airplane. When the airship was attacked, it would release its own airplane for protection. No practical results were achieved before the war ended. Here an English biplane, the Sopwith "Camel," a pursuit ship, has just left its "mother" airship.

Balloon Jumping

For some time balloon jumping was a popular fad. The lifting power of the balloon just about equalized the weight of the passenger, who thus could make long jumps with little effort. But in a strong wind such jumps were difficult to control, and coming down near high-tension wires was always hazardous. Shown below is the lady jumper, Emilie Sannom, preparing to go aloft, then descending (1931).

RIGHT: *Accounts of balloon trips always have reader appeal. This photograph shows the Swiss aeronaut Spelterini setting out for a flight accompanied by reporters from three leading Copenhagen newspapers.*

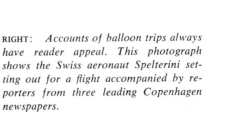

The Bennett international balloon races were annual events for a number of years. They were held in the United States several times until, after three victories by Demuyter of Belgium, the trophy went permanently to his country. Here the 1926 competitors are about to be sent off.

A balloon floats over the many spires in the Danish capital.

Heading Again for the North Pole

As mentioned before, Robert Peary reached the North Pole in 1909. After that, this inaccessible point lost some of its attraction, though much remained to be explored in the far north.

The illustrious explorer Roald Amundsen, who had reached the South Pole on December 12, 1911, decided sometime later to return to the Northern Hemisphere and undertake an expedition to the North Pole by airship. In 1926 he bought a new Italian airship that had been designed by, and built under the supervision of, Colonel Umberto Nobile. He engaged Nobile as chief pilot. When the Pole was finally reached, an Italian flag in honor of Nobile, an American flag in honor of the American millionaire Lincoln Ellsworth, who partly financed the expedition, and a Norwegian flag were dropped together onto the tangle of huge ice formations.

The remainder of this airship journey was most dramatic. Big sheets of ice formed on the cover of the hull, and when ice also formed on the propellers and was broken loose by centrifugal force, the heavy lumps were flung against the hull and damaged the cover. The radio ceased to function; the sun compass was covered with ice and could not be used, and so it was impossible to determine their position. Yet they managed to land the "Norge"—as it had been named—safely at Nome after a voyage of 3,400 miles.

The calm Scandinavian Amundsen and the excitable Italian Nobile were completely different in temperament. As a result of their experiences and reactions on the air voyage they had shared, they became bitter enemies.

Umberto Nobile, photographed before the takeoff of this airship built to his design.

LEFT: *The citizens of Oslo admire the "Norge" as it circles the capital.*

The "Norge" in front of the shed at Spitsbergen.

155

Nobile
Goes It Alone

Nobile noted the acclaim given Amundsen after the successful North Pole trip. Meanwhile, he himself had been promoted to the rank of general, and now he became determined to head his own expedition to the Polar regions. Financial support came from many quarters, as it was felt that the prestige of Mussolini and his fascist government would be enhanced if an Italian officer explored the remaining unknown areas in the Arctic.

Nobile's airship, "Italia," was of the same type and construction as the "Norge," but it could carry an additional 2,865 pounds. When it left Milan on April 15, 1928, Mussolini attended the ceremonies in person in spite of a recent attempt on his life.

The "Italia" arrived at Spitsbergen on May 6.

Before the airship left Milan, Cardinal Tosi blessed a cross donated by the Pope, to be dropped at the North Pole.

General Umberto Nobile with his fox terrier Titina in his arm. This dog was soon to be more in the limelight than any other dog in the world.

The "Italia" at New Aalesund prior to her departure on the polar flight.

Disaster in the Arctic Wasteland

The first part of the program was completed according to schedule. Islands off the Russian coast and in the Canadian archipelago were mapped, and then the course was set for the North Pole, which "Italia" crossed at midnight on May 24. It was an emotional moment marked by solemn ceremonies. One was the dropping of the Pope's cross, though fog prevailed at the time.

Nobile had intended to stay at the Pole for three weeks, but this idea was abandoned. Early the next morning, the course was set for Kingsbay on Spitsbergen.

Winds of near-hurricane strength soon began to blow, and "Italia" could make little headway. Simultaneously, new dangers appeared, among them the formation of ice, and by ten o'clock in the morning the airship could no longer sustain this additional weight. It hit the surface ice with great force. The impact partly crushed the control car and one of the engine nacelles—and the ten men stationed there, Nobile being one of them, were flung onto the ice. Relieved of their weight, the airship rose again with the six men who were in the undamaged engine nacelle. These men were never seen again.

One crew member was killed when the airship smashed down onto the ice, so only nine survivors remained. They immediately pitched camp on a drifting ice floe, for it turned out providentially that everything they required had dropped onto the ice with them—a tent, sleeping bags, a radio, and the necessary batteries for sixty hours of sending time, as well as numerous instruments. Even Nobile's dog Titina turned up unharmed. The tent was red; in addition to providing protection against the icy blasts, it would (it was hoped) furnish a conspicuous spot of color that rescuers could see.

The men lost no time in erecting the radio sender and beginning to send messages, but not until ten days later did a Russian radio fan pick up Nobile's SOS. Only then did the outside world learn that Nobile and some members of the expedition were alive and drifting on an ice floe. By that time, a great number of rescue expeditions of various kinds had already been organized.

An Italian vessel, City of Milan, *was one of those responding to the call for help from the drifting ice floe.*

LEFT: *More than twenty aircraft from several countries began an intense search for the survivors of the Nobile expedition. The Swedish lieutenant Einar Lundborg, one of the pilots engaged in this dangerous work, is seen here in front of his Fokker airplane at Hinlopen Strait. Lundborg was to play a dramatic part in the long-lasting North Pole disaster.*

Nobile's camp on the drifting ice floe, as seen from the air.

RIGHT: *Amundsen was among the first to volunteer to help search for Nobile and his men, in spite of the enmity between them since their earlier trip. He left Tromsö on June 18 as a passenger and observer in a French flying boat that had gone to Norway to join the hunt. That was the last ever seen of him. The aircraft must have encountered trouble in spite of its successful takeoff. When that ship disappeared, a still more extensive air search was launched. Here, Amundsen stands in front of the flying boat just before takeoff.*

LEFT: *The camp on the drifting ice floe. Red canvas had been selected for the tent, to make it easily visible from the air.*

159

A Rescuer Also Becomes
Stranded on the Ice

Nobile and his men waited impatiently on the drifting ice floe, for they knew that air rescue attempts were in the offing. However, many June days passed before anyone spotted the little red dot, their tent, in the vast wasteland of ice, and they were frequently downhearted.

Only six of the nine survivors now remained on the ice floe. Three men, the Swedish doctor Finn Malmgren and two Italians, Mariano and Zappi, had left on May 30 in an attempt to cross the drifting ice and reach solid ground on the continent farther south. But the strain told on the injured and exhausted Malmgren. When he could stand it no longer, he was left to die in an ice cavern.

Finally things began to happen. On June 20, Lieutenant Lundborg, the Swedish pilot, succeeded in making a skillful landing there with his Fokker, which was quite an achievement. His plane was a two-seater, so Lundborg could carry only one passenger on the return flight. He selected Nobile, and thereby opened another chapter in the tragedy of the Italian general. Many people—even Mussolini himself—disapproved of Nobile's behavior. They felt that, like the master of a ship, Nobile should have been the last to be rescued.

Lundborg promised to return promptly to fetch the rest of the stranded men, but his luck ran out. His plane hit an ice barrier and overturned when he came back a second time. Now he too was imprisoned on the ice.

On July 6 another aircraft succeeded in landing on the drifting floe. The pilot this time was Lieutenant Schyberg, also Swedish, and he had specific instructions to pick up his fellow pilot, Lundborg. By this time the ice had become too soft to risk more landings, and when Schyberg's small sport-type plane took off, the five Italians left behind realized that no more attempts would be made to rescue them by air. Later, they were picked up by the Russian icebreaker *Krassin,* which reached them after locating Mariano and Zappi en route and picking them up first. These two men had stayed together after leaving Malmgren behind. He succumbed to starvation and the intense cold.

Gradually the sad score of this disaster was complete. Roald Amundsen had vanished, along with the rest of the crew in his flying boat. In addition to Malmgren, seven other men from the Italian expedition had perished, and another search airplane had crashed with a loss of four lives.

The aftermath of the tragedy was to stay with Nobile a long time. An Italian committee was convened to investigate the affair, and after sixty sessions it decided unanimously that Nobile had been responsible for the disaster. However, he was never given a chance to testify in his own defense.

Nobile emigrated to Russia, and was placed in charge of that country's airship-building activities, participating in expeditions with airships of his own design. Not until toward the end of the 1930s was he permitted to return to his native country and was tolerated there.

Nobile was also injured when the airship crashed onto the ice. He is here seen being assisted to Lundborg's rescue plane.

RIGHT: *When Lundborg landed on the ice floe a second time, his plane overturned and he too became stranded. Some of the group awaiting rescue pose with his plane.*

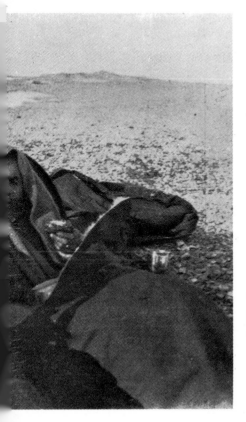

ABOVE: *Lieutenant Lundborg posed beside Nobile to have his picture taken as a souvenir of the occasion. He is holding Nobile's Titina. Nobile is resting in his sleeping bag.*

During Lundborg's stay on the ice floe, food and other welcome items were airdropped to him, such as this card, which would delight a collector of airmail memorabilia. It brought greetings from fellow members of the Swedish air rescue expedition.

On their return trip from the North Pole disaster, the surviving members of the expedition were photographed during a stop at the Mjölby railroad station in Sweden. Nobile's omnipresent dog Titina naturally did not miss the opportunity of getting into the picture.

161

Professor Piccard

The free balloon, drifting with the wind, remained well suited for scientific research, and during the 1930s the Swiss professor, Auguste Piccard, won fame using it to ascend into the stratosphere. To this end, he had a special, elongated balloon built. The totally enclosed, ball-shaped car made of aluminum could withstand great altitudes.

The first ascension was made from Augsburg, Germany, on May 27, 1931. Piccard and his assistant, Paul Kipfer, kept taking readings until they reached an altitude of over 51,000 feet.

On August 18 of the following year, with Max Cosyn as his scientific assistant, Piccard made a second balloon ascension into the stratosphere, this time reaching the still greater altitude of 54,000 feet.

Professor Piccard (right) *and his assistand, Paul Kipfer, just prior to their ascension. Both wear special crash helmets for head protection.*

OPPOSITE: *The Piccard balloon shortly before the takeoff from Augsburg. It is not fully filled because the hydrogen will expand in the lower air pressure of the higher altitudes.*

LEFT: *The first balloon ascension into the stratosphere lasted twenty-four hours. The landing occurred on the Gurgl glacier in the Italian Alps. Recovery of the balloon was hard work. Here mountain guides struggle to move the car toward where more adequate transportation is available.*

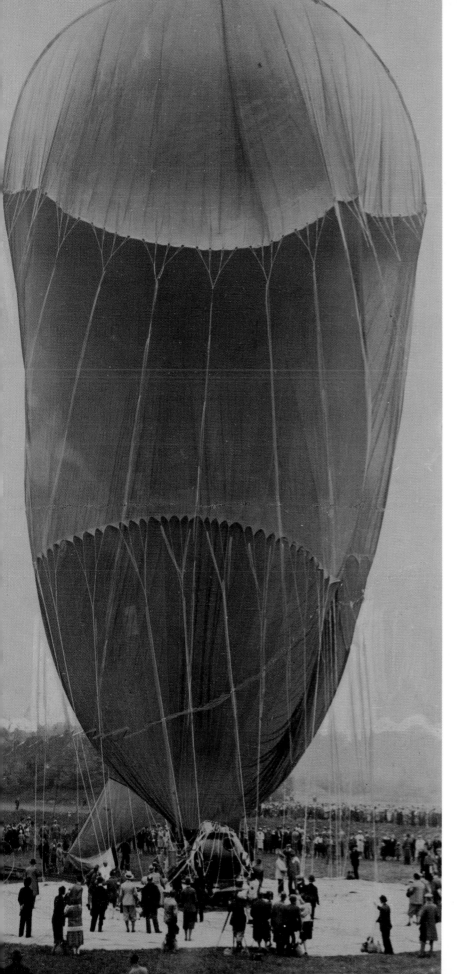

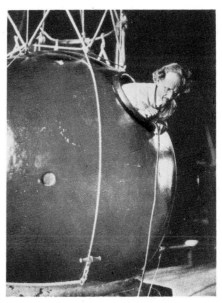

Piccard peers out of the hatch of the ball-shaped metal car.

Piccard was a professor at the University of Brussels, and Belgium commemorated his record ascension with a stamp issue of two denominations.

163

"Stratostat Calling—Conditions Serious . . ."

Auguste Piccard's record was not to remain uncontested for long. In 1933, a Soviet balloon with three men on board reached an altitude of 59,000 feet, and the following year the Russians set out to improve their own record.

This time their luck ran out. At an altitude of nearly 69,000 feet, the car broke away from the balloon. There was a radio on board, and horrified listeners on the ground heard the final message: "Stratostat calling—conditions serious—situation hopeless." An instant later, the car plunged to the ground, killing all on board.

A Russian balloon in 1933 set a world's record for altitude.

The large Russian balloon being filled with hydrogen in 1933.

A similar fate almost befell the American balloon "Explorer I" when it was used in an attempt to beat the previous altitude record. At an altitude of 59,000 feet the crew members, Captains Stevens and Anderson and Major Kepner, noticed that a horizontal tear had developed in the balloon cover and that one of the lines supporting the car had torn loose. The tear in the cover kept growing larger. Soon the balloon was almost useless except for its ability to function as a parachute.

The car also had an attached parachute, which could be released independently, but the crew decided to bide their time. If the situation became desperate, each one would use the individual parachute he wore. At around 20,000 feet the men managed to open the hatches, and when the balloon fabric shortly afterward blew apart into a multitude of small pieces, the three men jumped, one by one, and reached the ground safely.

This nerve-wracking experience did not deter Stevens and Anderson, who ascended the next year in a new balloon named "Explorer II" and reached the highest altitude yet—72,000 feet.

ABOVE, LEFT: *"Explorer I" ascending in 1934. The balloon was only partly filled at takeoff. Not until it reached a very high altitude would the hydrogen expand sufficiently to fill it.*

ABOVE, RIGHT: *Disaster struck at an altitude of 59,000 feet when the balloon fabric tore. The crew of three faced total destruction of their craft.*

A year after their difficult experience with "Explorer I," Captain Orvil Anderson and Captain Albert Stevens posed in front of the car from "Explorer II," in which they reached an altitude of 72,000 feet.

Big British Airships

When World War I ended, England dreamed of becoming the leading power in the air just as she had been on the seas. Airplanes were in their infancy; heavier-than-air craft still had only a limited range. So it was natural for England to turn to the airship, in the hope that it would provide her a link with her far-flung colonies.

In the last years of the war, several Zeppelins had been downed in England in fairly intact condition, so that they could be copied. The English models were ready when the war ended. One of them, "R 34," made the first double air crossing of the Atlantic—to New York and return. ("R" stands for "rigid.") Thereafter, work progressed on three larger airships, but it suffered a severe setback when one, "R 38," to be taken over by the United States government, broke up during a turning maneuver on a trial run above the Humber, with the loss of 44 lives.

Nonetheless, when Germany resumed large-scale airship activities, England was determined not to be left behind. The British government ordered two giant airships built with a capacity of nearly 5,000,000 cubic feet. Completed in 1929, they were considered by many to be the acme of technical achievement in airship construction. But all was not as perfect as it appeared. "R 101," the government-built airship for which the Air Ministry was responsible, proved to have a number of defects. When these had been corrected, it set out on a maiden voyage to India.

The contract for "R 100" had been awarded to a private concern, and it was the better airship. Its first extended voyage was a trip to Canada, and back to England. Both airships could accommodate 100 passengers and were outfitted with dining rooms, saloons, cabins, and a galley.

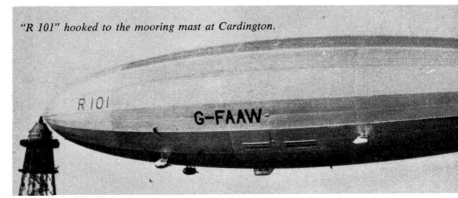

"R 101" hooked to the mooring mast at Cardington.

One of the giant English airships ready to take off while thousands crowd below to watch. The hull contains about 5,000,000 cubic feet of hydrogen.

A mooring mast was erected at Cardington for the two huge airships. The crowd is assembled below "R 100."

Disaster and National Tragedy

India was scheduled to be the first stop for "R 101," but disaster struck again—the ship hit the ground at Beauvais in France a short time after takeoff. The hydrogen burst into flames when "R 101" smashed into the ground, and soon nothing was left but the red-hot skeleton framework of dural. There had been fifty-four on board. Six miraculously escaped with their lives; the rest perished. Among the victims were the British Air Minister, Lord Thompson, and the designer of "R 101," Major Richmond.

This tragedy was felt as a national calamity. It signaled the end of large-scale airship activities in England—no more giant airships were built there. The companion airship "R 100" remained in service only one more year. Then it was dismantled.

An era had ended in England.

RIGHT: *After the disaster a court of inquiry investigated what little evidence remained. This picture shows the opening session. (Note the airship model on display.) It proved impossible to fix the cause of the disaster or determine the blame for the defects. The tragedy was attributed to a combination of unfortunate circumstances beyond human control.*

The Twilight of Giant Airships

In 1927, when the Allies repealed their prohibition of airship building and operation in Germany, the Germans began a new and larger airship in a giant shed at the Zeppelin works in Friedrichshafen, on Lake Constance.

170

Count Zeppelin had died in 1917. By then, he had already realized that his airships could no longer influence the course of the war. However, he lived long enough to become convinced of their usefulness as passenger carriers where long distances were to be covered, even though they seemed unsuited for war use.

When World War I drew to an end, fourteen Zeppelin airships still remained intact. Seven of these were destroyed by their own crews to prevent their falling into the hands of the Allies; the other seven were distributed as war booty among England, France, Italy, Belgium, and Japan. Thereafter, airship activities were at a standstill in Germany until the prohibition was lifted in 1927 and the Germans were permitted to carry on their proud tradition.

A giant new construction shed was erected at Friedrichshafen on Lake Constance, and work began on an airship that was to be larger than any previous Zeppelin and was to bear the name of the Count. This "Graf Zeppelin" was over 770 feet in length, weighed 117 tons, and could carry 20 passengers and a crew of 40.

A postcard paying homage to Count Zeppelin when all Germany went wild about him.

When Count Zeppelin died in 1917, he was given a state funeral. Here a rigid airship, his creation, passes above his funeral procession as a tribute of last respect.

The "Graf Zeppelin"

When it was completed in 1928, the "Graf Zeppelin" was admired all over the world—and justifiably. It was fitted with five engines of 530 horsepower each, and attained an hourly speed of 80 miles. The gasbags contained over 3,700,000 cubic feet of hydrogen.

There were plenty of tasks for the new Zeppelin to tackle, and a number of voyages to distant countries had been planned. It crossed the Atlantic on its first long trip in October 1928. The following year, "Graf Zep" (as it was commonly called) demonstrated its airworthiness by circumnavigating the globe in twenty days.

In 1931, the "Graf Zeppelin" crossed the ice fields at the North Pole, following the route covered by "Norge" and "Italia." Next, it flew over the pyramids in Egypt, and before many more months had passed, it further proved its mettle by settling down to the everyday task of making regular crossings back and forth to Brazil with mail and passengers.

Still, every trip of this giant craft remained news that papers all over the world found it worthwhile to report.

Stores are brought on board the "Graf Zeppelin."

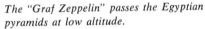

The "Graf Zeppelin" passes the Egyptian pyramids at low altitude.

Check-in time, on the "Graf."

RIGHT: "Graf Zep" over the Statue of Liberty on her maiden voyage to the United States.

Weight at a Premium

The "Graf Zeppelin" was admired not least for her accommodations, which were luxurious for that day. Weight was of prime importance, down to the last item—even provisions were no exception. Though the great craft was a far cry from the first balloons that followed the whim of the winds, the fundamentals remained basically unchanged: in lighter-than-air travel, *everything* had to be as light as possible.

The dining room in the "Graf Zeppelin" mixed modern styles and the fashions of grandfather's time. The chairs were so light that they could be balanced on one finger.

BELOW: *There was always much to observe on crossings in clear weather. On this trip the passengers could see a steamer stranded off Gibraltar.*

Passengers had a choice of amusements. Chess was played on a lightweight board.

postcard showing the "Graf" over Cairo ould be mailed from the post office on oard.

Limited galley space but wonderful meals.

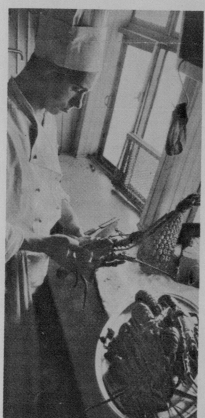

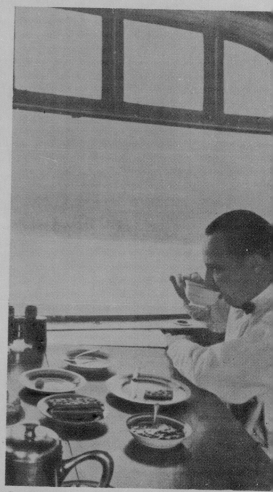

Captain Lehmann enjoys a marvelous view while breakfasting.

The 200-Ton "Hindenburg"

The "Hindenburg," surpassing the "Graf Zeppelin" and the English "R 100" and "R 101" in size, was ready for its trial run in March of 1936. Its capacity was better than 6,700,000 cubic feet; it weighed nearly 200 tons and had a speed of nearly 85 miles an hour. Fifty passengers could be accommodated in its cabins, dining halls, lavatories, lounges, and other facilities, which were arranged in two stories. There was a crew of 40.

This newest air giant made headlines everywhere. After its trial runs, it entered regular transatlantic service between Germany and the U.S.A.

Giant airships remained news even after transatlantic operations became common. "Hindenburg" successfully crossed the North Atlantic twenty times.

ABOVE: *The completed "Hindenburg" in the shed on Lake Constance.*

GAS TEMPERATURE

AIR TEMPERATURE

ALTIMETER

Germany's latest giant airships were shown in the air together before cheering crowds in Berlin. This photograph has an almost sinister implication—in the foreground is the Brandenburg Gate, the symbol of German power.

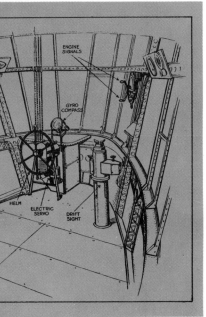

Every transatlantic crossing of the "Hindenburg" was a newsworthy event, though by May 1937 the ship had made a full score of such voyages. On the twenty-first crossing Birger Brinck, a reporter for the *Copenhagen Politiken* and the *Stockholm Tidningen*, was a passenger. His last message read:

We are now approaching our goal. This is my final cablegram from the airship prior to our landing. An hour ago we passed over Boston. We crossed this city at a low altitude, and the vessels in the harbor saluted us by blowing their whistles. This last hour has been one continuous fantastic experience. We are following Long Island Sound, but it is so foggy we have had to climb above the clouds. Everywhere our eyes dwell upon a fairy landscape of fog that assumes varying aspects as the sun plays upon it. We cannot see the country below us, but Captain Pruss has promised us that he will let the airship dive below the fog as we approach New York so that we may enjoy her skyscrapers.

The End of an Era

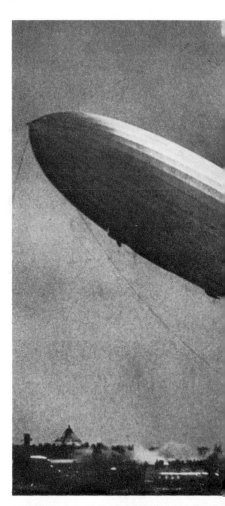

One hour after the dispatch of the cablegram about the progress of "Hindenburg" toward New York, newspapers around the world received this shocking message: "GERMANY'S PRIDE, THE ZEPPELIN HINDENBURG, EXPLODED WHILE LANDING IN NEW YORK."

One of the reporters present at Lakehurst gave this eyewitness account of the disaster to the *Copenhagen Politiken:*

When "Hindenburg" approached, I was walking on the concrete runway of the Lakehurst airport with Dr. Armandus Johnson and Daily News aviation editor Duke Krantz. The heavy downpour forced us to seek shelter in a car almost directly below the airship, and we were there when the first explosion occurred. It was 7:20 P.M. (local time, or 20 minutes past midnight, European time). We were almost ejected from the car, and had to run to save our lives while being showered by burning parts from the airship.

When "Hindenburg" was about 380 yards away from the mooring mast the engines were stopped, and the airship then descended slowly. At this moment the explosion occurred. It started amidships, and was immediately followed by another explosion aft. More now followed in rapid succession. They sounded like strong cannon shots, but immediately after the first explosion the airship was transformed into a sea of flames. "Hindenburg" buckled and the stern started to drop.

We saw passengers at this moment begin to jump from the airship to escape the flames. They fell helter-skelter on the ground. Some tried to crawl away, others remained motionless and unconscious. It was a terrifying sight.

This disaster caused a greater stir than previous air accidents, not only because the "Hindenburg" had been destroyed and thirty-six men and women killed, but also because it now became self-evident that airships were not the solution to mass air transportation. More than "Hindenburg" vanished—an era ended as well.

Afterward, much criticism was expressed that nonflammable helium had not been used for filling the airship instead of hydrogen, but it was claimed that it had proved impossible for Germany to buy helium in the United States, the only country then producing it. Later, it came out that Germany could have bought American helium, but the German government felt it could not spare the required foreign exchange.

The "Graf" was retired a few months after the "Hindenburg" disaster. During the succeeding two years more than a million visitors inspected it in one of the airship sheds at Rhine-Main airport.

Work on a third airship had commenced prior to the loss of the "Hindenburg," and the name "Graf Zeppelin" was to have been transferred to this airship. It made its maiden voyage on September 14, 1938, but by then purchasing helium in the United States was practically impossible to arrange. So this third giant airship was never used to any extent.

Airplanes attacking an observation kite balloon.

During World War I, kite balloons were used extensively for artillery observation by both the Allies and the enemy. But balloons of this type proved extremely vulnerable, and they have since been superseded by other aircraft even though modern kite balloons are now motorized and hence are practically small dirigible airships.

It might be said that World War II captive balloons fought back at their attackers: barrage balloons caught in their nets enemy aircraft that tried to sneak in undetected beneath the protecting radar screens.

K-type kite balloon, which can be motorized and operated like an airship. The fin, rudder, and elevator are then added. The car holds a crew of three. Here it is shown on Danish army maneuvers.

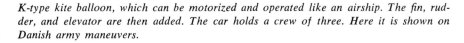

The officer is ready to go aloft to make observations. His parachute hangs outside the car, ready for use if needed. The photograph dates from 1932.

This compact motor winch for use with kite balloons could move across rough terrain.

181

The Second World War

At the start of World War II, almost all the warring countries had captive balloons for observation purposes. It soon became evident that they, like airships, had gradually become inferior to airplanes. They proved far too vulnerable to attack by fighter aircraft.

Yet airships were not to be completely relegated to the junkyard. In America particularly, they were found to be useful as submarine hunters and convoy escorts. The initial United States naval fleet of eight blimps grew to 150 in the course of the war.

The captive balloon achieved its greatest importance as a barrier against bomber planes and rockets. All the southeastern corner of England gradually was made "Verboten Territory" by means of a curtain of 2,000 such balloons. It was largely due to the barrier balloons that only 29 percent of the German V-bombs reached London.

A few of the 2,000 barrier balloons that protected England in World War II, shown here in an airship shed.

A 1940 view of an English barrier balloon with observation car, falling in flames.

182

A German captive balloon being filled with gas on the Western Front at the beginning of World War II. This modern-style captive balloon served the combined purposes of providing observation facilities and acting as a barrier against enemy airplanes.

The captive balloon rises after being filled with gas.

A New Atlantic Crossing

Crossing the Atlantic by airship had become pretty common, but nobody had succeeded in going by air from the New World to the Old, or vice versa, in an old-fashioned balloon. In fact, except for the attempts of John Wise in 1873 and Walter Wellman in 1910, no one else had intentionally ventured far out to sea in a balloon until four daring English aeronauts came along who had enough courage to make the attempt. They were the fifty-one-year-old Arnold "Bushy" Eiloart, his twenty-one-year-old son Tim, and the couple Colin and Rosemary Mudie, age thirty-two and thirty, respectively.

This little group left the Canary Islands on December 12, 1958. They managed to stay in the air with their balloon for almost ninety-six hours before being forced to come down in the Atlantic. However, their balloon car was fitted out as a boat, and it fortunately proved seaworthy. Though they suffered badly from thirst on the way, they finally reached the West Indies on January 5, 1959.

Their balloon, "The Small World," got into trouble after being caught by a strong updraft. To counterbalance this, they valved hydrogen for so long that the balloon could no longer maintain altitude, although they threw out all the ballast that could be spared—even their radio and other important equipment.

National Geographic Magazine *printed a map of this balloon trip, the first four days of which were spent in the air, the remaining twenty on the water.*

West Indies

Caribbean Sea

Barbados

1,500 nautical miles in 20 days

Balloon flight ended after 1,200 nautical miles

TRADE WINDS pushed balloon at 10 to 15 m.p.h.

SOUTH AMERICA

Atlantic Ocean

AFRICA

OPPOSITE: *The four aeronauts before their departure. From left, they are Colin and Rosemary Mudie, Tim and Arnold Eiloart.*

Aeronaut Arnold "Bushy" Eiloart becomes a seafaring pilot.

RIGHT: National Geographic *pictured "The Small World" above the billowing waves of the Atlantic.*

A "Lady Landing"

As mentioned frequently, balloon ascensions long remained popular at Copenhagen's Tivoli Gardens. After an interval without any, ascensions were planned to mark the hundred-and-twenty-fifth anniversary of the world-famous park. To celebrate the occasion in fitting style, among those engaged were the Dutch balloonists Nini and Jan Boesman, who had made ascensions in many parts of the world.

The Boesmans' trip was pleasant and successful. As often happens on ascensions from Tivoli, the balloon was carried to southern Sweden because west winds predominate in Denmark. When they descended, motorists pursued them, ready to grasp the drag rope and hold the car after pulling it down to what is, in the parlance of balloonists, a "lady landing."

The poster advertising this event used the old-style layout of such announcements.

Filling the balloon in Tivoli Gardens.

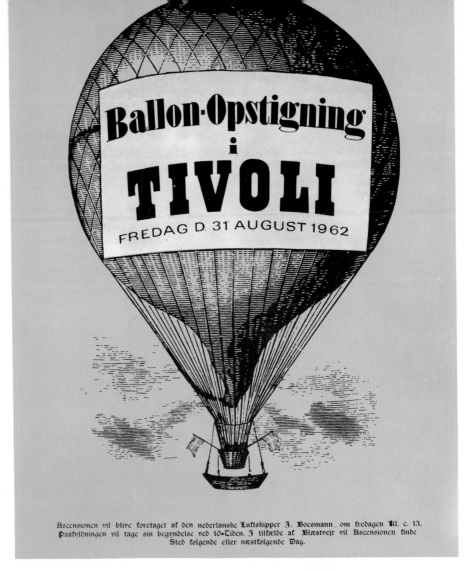

Ballon-Opstigning i TIVOLI

FREDAG D. 31 AUGUST 1962

Ascensionen vil blive foretaget af den nederlanske Luftskipper J. Boesmann om fredagen Kl. c. 13. Paafyldningen vil tage sin begyndelse ved 10-Tiden. I tilfælde af Blæstvejr vil Ascensionen finde Sted følgende eller næstfølgende Dag.

A balloon ascension can be a beautiful sight.
The exotic-looking foreground adds special
interest here—but the building is actually
the Chinese Tower restaurant at Tivoli,
rather than in some city of the Far East.

187

An Unrivaled View of Four Countries

Keen balloon pilots all over the world keep their fascinating sport active. International competitions are held annually. Alpine balloon rallies, for example, have been held in the Swiss town of Mürren since 1962. Participants that year were such balloon veterans as the French air historian Charles Dollfus; the Dutch couple, the Boesmans (he manages the balloon museum in The Hague); English pilots Anthony Smith and Gerry Turnbull; and the Swiss Fred Dolder.

Mürren rallies offer the attraction of crossing the Alps in majestic silence while viewing four adjoining countries. Nor are dramatic incidents lacking. For instance, Nini Boesman—one of the few woman balloon pilots—was surprised by unpredictable winds over the Rhone valley and made a descent that by no stretch of the imagination could be called a "lady landing"—one where the balloon car comes to rest right side up and it is not even necessary to pull the rip cord. Mrs. Boesman had to alight among trees on a mountain.

Swiss poster for the first international Alpine balloon rally.

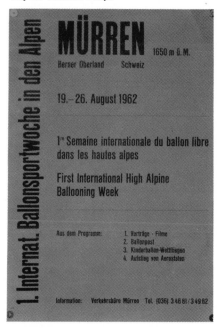

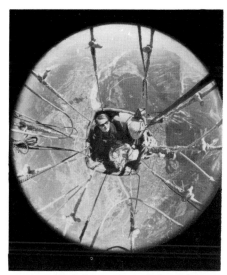

The broadcaster carries on a running commentary while a German club balloon is being filled prior to attaching its basket.

The Balloon Today

The balloon remains a unique and integral part of modern life even though ascensions are now rare events. The movies, for example, have revived all the balloon stories of Jules Verne and other writers. And balloons figure in comic strips and in advertisements, trademarks, and elsewhere.

The balloon was man's first vehicle of the air—and as such it continues to fascinate us. Possibly it is the female touch to the shape of the balloon that strikes a tender note.

An insurance company advertisement uses a balloon as a symbol of safety.

Most of the movies based on Jules Verne's prophetic tales treat the subject seriously, but a couple have been humorous. In These Flying Fools, *Dalia Lahvi is subjected to a watery treatment on her honeymoon with her ballooning husband.*

EL CAPITAN TRUENO

en

¡UN AJEDREZ SINIESTRO!

REVISTA PARA LOS

Comic strips often resort to a balloon for escapes. In this Spanish comic, courageous Captain Trueno helps a beautiful girl flee in his balloon.

There are records of odd accidents in the annals of ballooning—on at least three occasions involving boys who were carried aloft involuntarily. One such mishap occurred in 1843 when a Montgolfière tore loose and went aloft without its pilot. The balloon anchor snagged a twelve-year-old boy named Guerin and carried him away, as shown at right. He came down safely when the hot air in the balloon cooled. Ralph Heron, an English boy, was not so lucky. In 1786, at Newcastle, he became entangled and fell to his death. The third accident befell an American boy, Danny Nowell (below), in 1964. His ride covered only 100 yards and his only injury was a sprained ankle.

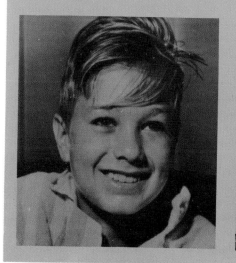

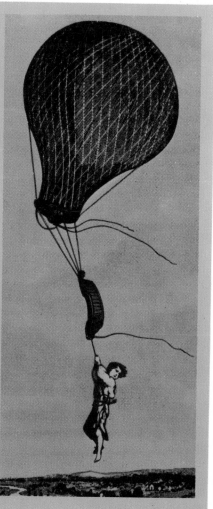

The more-than-a-century-old tradition of balloon ascensions at Tivoli Gardens was revived in 1968 to celebrate the hundred-and-twenty-fifth anniversary of that establishment. Among the pilots engaged was Don Piccard, American balloon manufacturer and a descendant of the Professor Piccard famed for flights into the stratosphere.

Don Piccard's balloon, like many others today, used a bottle-gas installation, a cheaper method than hydrogen or illuminating gas. It makes the filling of balloons independent of the availability of gas pipes.

The anniversary celebration was also marked by a display of balloon documents and souvenirs from the collection of this translator, to show the development of airmail. In 1808 Denmark's first aeronaut, Johan Peter Colding, made the earliest airmail experiments, sending small balloons bearing messages addressed to the Danish king, who supported Colding's activities, across the Belt waters between the two largest Danish islands. Some of these missives are preserved in the government archives of Denmark and the Public Records of the British Admiralty

Two views of the filling of a modern hot-air balloon on the occasion of Don Piccard's ascent.

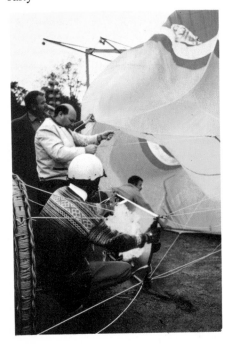

The face side of an 1808 Colding air letter addressed to His Majesty King Frederic VI, Copenhagen Headquarters. This first recorded airmail bears the notation "Carried across the Great Belt in an aerostatic machine."

A modern hot-air balloon with plastic cover uses bottle gas to heat the air above by means of a burner installed in the car below.

LEFT: *Colorful posters, like this one from Tivoli, which is sought by poster collectors, remain one of the most effective means of attracting visitors.*

RIGHT: *The Ferris wheel is a popular attraction in most amusement parks. A wheel of the balloon variety at Tivoli Gardens has delighted young and old for years. Here some of the dancers and performers at the park, in their fancy dresses, occupy one of the cars.*

Aeronautic souvenirs are favorites with collectors, and old items showing balloons command high prices. Real connoisseurs, however, take pains to study the history of aeronautics. The specimens here, from an indiscriminate collection, show little regard for facts. The artists display more imagination than knowledge of actual balloon ascensions. There were none as early as 1718, as the picture at left would have us believe. We know now that Montgolfière, Charles, and Robert did not go up until 1783.

The drawing at right might be suitable for the Travelers Insurance Company—if we wanted to speculate on who commissioned it. More likely, however, the artist had read something about Nadar's "Giant," and thereafter gave free rein to his imagination.

195

A Modern Reenactment

Today, ballooning is still popular—more ascensions are made annually than in the year when ballooning commenced. This monumental event in man's long conquest of the air was reenacted in 1951 in the Bois de Boulogne with a replica of the Montgolfière in which the undaunted Pilâtre de Rozier and D'Arlandes went aloft on November 21, 1783, cheered by multitudes of enthusiastic onlookers. The spectators at the 1951 takeoff wore costumes of the eighteenth century. All the illustrations on this page are photos taken of the reenactment.

Serenity and Tragedy

The grim commentary is made that few fatal accidents occur in the air; that danger lurks only in the takeoff and landing. This comment can be applied to ballooning. However, even the skilled balloon pilot can be confronted with situations where he misjudges distances and collides with an obstacle. Or a sudden treacherous gust of wind may upset his calculations.

That was how the experienced balloon pilot Robert Trauger came to grief in 1968 when he ascended from Pennel, Pennsylvania, with a woman passenger, Joanna Flannery. The hot-air balloon collided with high tension wires and caught fire. Both pilot and passenger were hurled out and plunged to their death. A photographer, Vincent Wilkersson, had his camera focused on the balloon and took a picture at the instant the tragedy occurred.

The serene, silent floating of the balloon holds pilot and passengers in its spell as they chase the shadow of the balloon across the landscape. The scene may be a moonlit night or a midsummer day such as the artist tried to show on the almanac cover at right. But balloonists are also attracted by the challenge to their presence of mind, meteorological knowledge, and skill.

Folkets Jul 1950

197

Man Still Needs a Source of Power

Man has learned how to rise from the ground and control his aircraft, but he has never learned to fly like a bird, using only his *own* power. Many have tried to make this age-old dream come true and have failed.

The conclusion of the astronomer Lalande in 1700 is still as valid as ever: "It has been proved that we human beings are incapable of rising from the ground and soaring in the air. . . . Why waste time on attempts at changing Nature's basic laws?"

However, man does not give up easily. That was particularly true in the case of the French inventor Lepine, shown below. He believed he had found the solution, yet was doomed to disappointment like other optimists before and after him.